The Essel

TRIUMPH

BONNEVILLE

Your marque expert: Peter Henshaw

VELOCE PUBLISHING
THE PUBLISHER OF FINE AUTOMOTIVE BOOKS

Also from Veloce Publishing

SpeedPro Series
4-Cylinder Engine – How to Blueprint & Build a Short Block for High Performance (Hammill)
Alfa Romeo DOHC High-Performance Manual (Kartalamakis)
Alfa Romeo V6 Engine High-Performance Manual (Kartalamakis)
BMC 998cc A-Series Engine – How to Power Tune (Hammill)
1275cc A-Series High-Performance Manual (Hammill)
Camshafts – How to Choose & Time them for Maximum Power (Hammill)
Cylinder Heads – How to Build, Modify & Power Tune Updated & Revised Edition (Burgess & Gollan)
Distributor-type Ignition Systems – How to Build & Power Tune (Hammill)
Fast Road Car – How to Plan and Build Revised & Updated Colour New Edition (Stapleton)
Ford SOHC 'Pinto' & Sierra Cosworth DOHC Engines – How to Power Tune Updated & Enlarged Edition (Hammill)
Ford V8 – How to Power Tune Small Block Engines (Hammill)
Harley-Davidson Evolution Engines – How to Build & Power Tune (Hammill)
Holley Carburetors – How to Build & Power Tune Revised & Updated Edition (Hammill)
Jaguar XK Engines – How to Power Tune Revised & Updated Colour Edition (Hammill)
MG Midget & Austin-Healey Sprite – How to Power Tune Updated & Revised Edition (Stapleton)
MGB 4-Cylinder Engine – How to Power Tune (Burgess)
MGB V8 Power – How to Give Your, Third Colour Edition (Williams)
MGB, MGC & MGB V8 – How to Improve (Williams)
Mini Engines – How to Power Tune on a Small Budget Colour Edition (Hammill)
Motorcycle-engined Racing Car – How to Build (Pashley)
Motorsport – Getting Started (Collins)
Motorsports Datalogging (Templeman)
Nitrous Oxide High-Performance Manual (Langfield)
Rover V8 Engines – How to Power Tune (Hammill)
Sportscar/Kitcar Suspension & Brakes – How to Build & Modify Enlarged & Updated 2nd Edition (Hammill)
SU Carburettor High-Performance Manual (Hammill)
Supercar, How to Build (Thompson)
Suzuki 4x4 – How to Modify for Serious Off-Road Action (Richardson)
Tiger Avon Sportscar – How to Build Your Own Updated & Revised 2nd Edition (Dudley)
TR2, 3 & TR4 – How to Improve (Williams)
TR5, 250 & TR6 – How to Improve (Williams)
TR7 & TR8, How to Improve (Williams)
V8 Engine – How to Build a Short Block for High Performance (Hammill)
Volkswagen Beetle Suspension, Brakes & Chassis – How to Modify for High Performance (Hale)
Volkswagen Bus Suspension, Brakes & Chassis – How to Modify for High Performance (Hale)
Weber DCOE, & Dellorto DHLA Carburetors – How to Build & Power Tune 3rd Edition (Hammill)

Those were the days ... Series
Alpine Trials & Rallies 1910-1973 (Pfundner)
Austerity Motoring (Bobbitt)
Brighton National Speed Trials (Gardiner)
British Police Cars (Walker)
British Woodies (Peck)
Crystal Palace by (Collins)
Dune Buggy Phenomenon (Hale)
Dune Buggy Phenomenon Volume 2 (Hale)
MG's Abingdon Factory (Moylan)
Motor Racing at Brands Hatch in the Seventies (Parker)
Motor Racing at Goodwood in the Sixties (Gardiner)
Motor Racing at Oulton Park in the 1960s (McFadyen)
Motor Racing at Oulton Park in the 1970s (McFadyen)
Short Oval Racing in the 1980s (Neil)
Three Wheelers (Bobbitt)

Enthusiast's Restoration Manual Series
Citroën 2CV, How to Restore (Porter)
Classic Car Bodywork, How to Restore (Thaddeus)
Classic Car Electrics (Thaddeus)
Classic Cars, How to Paint (Thaddeus)
Reliant Regal, How to Restore (Payne)
Triumph TR2/3/3A, How to Restore (Williams)
Triumph TR4/4A, How to Restore (Williams)
Triumph TR5/250 & 6, How to Restore (Williams)
Triumph TR7/8, How to Restore (Williams)
Volkswagen Beetle, How to Restore (Tyler)
VW Bay Window Bus (Paxton)
Yamaha FS1-E, How to Restore (Watts)

Essential Buyer's Guide Series
Alfa GT (Booker)
Alfa Romeo Spider Giulia (Booker & Talbott)
BMW GS (Henshaw)
BSA Bantam (Henshaw)
BSA Twins (Henshaw)
Citroën 2CV (Paxton)
Citroën ID & DS (Heilig)
Fiat 500 & 600 (Bobbitt)
Jaguar E-type 3.8 & 4.2-litre (Crespin)
Jaguar E-type V12 5.3-litre (Crespin)
Jaguar/Daimler XJ6, XJ12 & Sovereign (Crespin)
Jaguar XJ-S (Crespin)
MGB & MGB GT (Williams)
Mercedes-Benz 280SL-560SL Roadsters (Bass)
Mercedes-Benz 'Pagoda' 230SL, 250SL & 280SL Roadsters & Coupés (Bass)
Morris Minor (Newell)
Porsche 928 (Hemmings)
Rolls-Royce Silver Shadow & Bentley T-Series (Bobbitt)
Subaru Impreza (Hobbs)
Triumph Bonneville (Henshaw)
Triumph TR6 (Williams)
VW Beetle (Cservenka & Copping)
VW Bus (Cservenka & Copping)

Auto-Graphics Series
Fiat-based Abarths (Sparrow)
Jaguar MkI & II Saloons (Sparrow)
Lambretta LI series scooters (Sparrow)

Rally Giants Series
Audi Quattro (Robson)
Big Healey – 100-Six & 3000 (Robson)
Ford Escort MkI (Robson)
Ford Escort RS1800 (Robson)
Lancia Stratos (Robson)
Peugeot 205 T16 (Robson)
Subaru Impreza (Robson)

General
1½-litre GP Racing 1961-1965 (Whitelock)
AC Two-litre Saloons & Buckland Sportscars (Archibald)
According to Carter (Skelton)
Alfa Romeo Giulia Coupé GT & GTA (Tipler)
Alfa Romeo Montreal - The Essential Companion (Taylor)
Alfa Tipo 33 (McDonough & Collins)
Anatomy of the Works Minis (Moylan)
Armstrong-Siddeley (Smith)
Autodrome (Collins & Ireland)
Automotive A-Z, Lane's Dictionary of Automotive Terms (Lane)
Automotive Mascots (Kay & Springate)
Bahamas Speed Weeks, The (O'Neil)
Bentley Continental, Corniche and Azure (Bennett)
Bentley MkVI, Rolls-Royce Silver Wraith, Dawn & Cloud/ Bentley R & S-series (Nutland)
BMC Competitions Department Secrets (Turner, Chambers & Browning)
BMW 5-Series (Cranswick)
BMW Z-Cars (Taylor)
British 250cc Racing Motorcycles by Chris Pereira
British Cars, The Complete Catalogue of, 1895-1975 (Culshaw & Horrobin)
BRM – a mechanic's tale (Salmon)
BRM V16 (Ludvigsen)
BSA Bantam Bible (Henshaw)
Bugatti Type 40 (Price)
Bugatti 46/50 Updated Edition (Price & Arbey)
Bugatti T44 & T49 (Price & Arbey)
Bugatti 57 2nd Edition (Price)
Caravans, The Illustrated History 1919-1959 (Jenkinson)
Caravans, The Illustrated History from 1960 (Jenkinson)
Carrera Panamericana (Tipler)
Chrysler 300 – America's Most Powerful Car 2nd Edition (Ackerson)
Chrysler PT Cruiser (Ackerson)
Citroën DS (Bobbitt)
Cliff Alison - From the Fells to Ferrari (Gauld)
Cobra – The Real Thing! (Legate)
Cortina – Ford's Bestseller (Robson)
Coventry Climax Racing Engines (Hammill)
Daimler SP250 New Edition (Long)
Datsun Fairlady Roadster to 280ZX – The Z-car Story (Long)
Dino – The V6 Ferrari (Long)
Dodge Charger – Enduring Thunder (Ackerson)
Dodge Dynamite! (Grist)
Draw & Paint Cars – How to (Gardiner)
Drive on the Wild Side, A – 20 extreme driving adventures from around the world (Weaver)
Ducati 750 Bible, The (Falloon)
Ducati 860, 900 and Mille Bible, The (Falloon)
Dune Buggy, Building a – The Essential Manual (Shakespeare)
Dune Buggy Files (Hale)
Dune Buggy Handbook (Hale)
Edward Turner: the man behind the motorcycles (Clew)
Fiat & Abarth 124 Spider & Coupé (Tipler)
Fiat & Abarth 500 & 600 2nd edition (Bobbitt)
Fiats, Great Small (Ward)
Fine Art of the Motorcycle Engine, The (Peirce)
Ford F100/F150 Pick-up 1948-1996 (Ackerson)
Ford F150 1997-2005 (Ackerson)
Ford GT – Then, and Now (Streather)
Ford GT40 (Legate)
Ford in Miniature (Olson)
Ford Model Y (Roberts)
Ford Thunderbird from 1954, The Book of the (Long)
Forza Minardi! (Vigar)
Funky Mopeds (Skelton)
Gentleman Jack (Gauld)
GM in Miniature (Olson)
GT – The World's Best GT Cars 1953-73 (Dawson)
Hillclimbing & Sprinting – The essential manual (Short & Wilkinson)
Honda NSX (Long)
Jaguar, The Rise of (Price)
Jaguar XJ-S (Long)
Jeep CJ (Ackerson)
Jeep Wrangler (Ackerson)
Karmann-Ghia Coupé & Convertible (Bobbitt)
Lambretta Bible, The (Davies)
Lancia 037 (Collins)
Lancia Delta HF Integrale (Blaettel & Wagner)
Land Rover, The Half-Ton Military (Cook)
Laverda Twins & Triples Bible 1968-1986 (Falloon)
Lea-Francis Story, The (Price)
Lexus Story, The (Long)
little book of smart, the (Jackson)
Lola – The Illustrated History (1957-1977) (Starkey)
Lola – All the Sports Racing & Single-Seater Racing Cars 1978-1997 (Starkey)
Lola T70 – The Racing History & Individual Chassis Record 3rd Edition (Starkey)
Lotus 49 (Oliver)
MarketingMobiles, The Wonderful Wacky World of (Hale)
Mazda MX-5/Miata 1.6 Enthusiast's Workshop Manual (Grainger & Shoemark)
Mazda MX-5/Miata 1.8 Enthusiast's Workshop Manual (Grainger & Shoemark)
Mazda MX-5 Miata: the book of the world's favourite sportscar (Long)
Mazda MX-5 Miata Roadster (Long)
MGA (Price Williams)
MGB & MGB GT – Expert Guide (Auto-Doc Series) (Williams)
MGB Electrical Systems (Astley)
Micro Caravans (Jenkinson)
Micro Trucks (Mort)
Microcars at large! (Quellin)
Mini Cooper – The Real Thing! (Tipler)
Mitsubishi Lancer Evo, the road car & WRC story (Long)
Montlhéry, the story of the Paris autodrome (Boddy)
Morgan Maverick (Lawrence)
Morris Minor, 60 years on the road (Newell)
Moto Guzzi Sport & Le Mans Bible (Falloon)
Motor Movies – The Posters! (Veysey)
Motor Racing – Reflections of a Lost Era (Carter)
Motorcycle Road & Racing Chassis Designs (Noakes)
Motorhomes, The Illustrated History (Jenkinson)
Motorsport in colour, 1950s (Wainwright)
Nissan 300ZX & 350Z – The Z-Car Story (Long)
Pass the Theory and Practical Driving Tests (Gibson & Hoole)
Peking to Paris 2007 (Young)
Plastic Toy Cars of the 1950s & 1960s (Ralston)
Pontiac Firebird (Cranswick)
Porsche Boxster (Long)
Porsche 356 (2nd edition) (Long)
Porsche 911 Carrera – The Last of the Evolution (Corlett)
Porsche 911R, RS & RSR, 4th Edition (Starkey)
Porsche 911 – The Definitive History 1963-1971 (Long)
Porsche 911 – The Definitive History 1971-1977 (Long)
Porsche 911 – The Definitive History 1977-1987 (Long)
Porsche 911 – The Definitive History 1987-1997 (Long)
Porsche 911 – The Definitive History 1997-2004 (Long)
Porsche 911SC 'Super Carrera' – The Essential Companion (Streather)
Porsche 914 & 914-6: The Definitive History Of The Road & Competition Cars (Long)
Porsche 924 (Long)
Porsche 944 (Long)
Porsche 993 'King of Porsche' – The Essential Companion (Streather)
Porsche 996 'Supreme Porsche' – The Essential Companion (Streather)
Porsche Racing Cars – 1953 to 1975 (Long)
Porsche Racing Cars – 1976 on (Long)
Porsche – The Rally Story (Meredith)
Porsche: Three Generations of Genius (Meredith)
RAC Rally Action! (Gardiner)
Rallye Sport Fords: the inside story (Moreton)
Redman, Jim – 6 Times World Motorcycle Champion: The Autobiography (Redman)
Rolls-Royce Silver Shadow/Bentley T Series Corniche & Camargue Revised & Enlarged Edition (Bobbitt)
Rolls-Royce Silver Spirit, Silver Spur & Bentley Mulsanne 2nd Edition (Bobbitt)
RX-7 – Mazda's Rotary Engine Sportscar (updated & revised new edition) (Long)
Scooters & Microcars, The A-Z of popular (Dan)
Scooter Lifestyle (Grainger)
Singer Story: Cars, Commercial Vehicles, Bicycles & Motorcycles (Atkinson)
SM – Citroën's Maserati-engined Supercar (Long & Claverol)
Subaru Impreza: the road car and WRC story (Long)
Taxi! The Story of the 'London' Taxicab (Bobbitt)
Tinplate Toy Cars of the 1950s & 1960s (Ralston)
Toyota Celica & Supra, The book of Toyota's Sports Coupés (Long)
Toyota MR2 Coupés & Spyders (Long)
Triumph Motorcycles & the Meriden Factory (Hancox)
Triumph Speed Twin & Thunderbird Bible (Woolridge)
Triumph Tiger Cub Bible (Estall)
Triumph Trophy Bible (Woolridge)
Triumph TR6 (Kimberley)
Unraced (Collins)
Velocette Motorcycles – MSS to Thruxton Updated & Revised (Burris)
Virgil Exner – Visioneer: The official biography of Virgil M Exner designer extraordinaire (Grist)
Volkswagen Bus Book, The (Bobbitt)
Volkswagen Bus or Van to Camper, How to Convert (Porter)
Volkswagens of the World (Glen)
VW Beetle Cabriolet (Bobbitt)
VW Beetle – The Car of the 20th Century (Copping)
VW Bus – 40 years of Splitties, Bays & Wedges (Copping)
VW Bus Book, The (Bobbitt)
VW Golf: five generations of fun (Copping & Cservenka)
VW – The air-cooled era (Copping)
VW T5 Camper Conversion Manual (Porter)
VW Campers (Copping)
Works Minis, The Last (Purves & Brenchley)
Works Rally Mechanic (Moylan)

First published in February 2008. Veloce Publishing Ltd., 33 Trinity Street, Dorchester DT1 1TT, England. Fax 01305 268864/e-mail veloce@veloce.co.uk/web www.veloce.co.uk
ISBN 978-1-84584-134-8/UPC 6-368470-4134-2

Readers with ideas for automotive books, or books on other transport or related hobby subjects, are invited to write to the editorial director of Veloce Publishing at the above address.
British Library Cataloguing in Publication Data – A catalogue record for this book is available from the British Library.
Typesetting, design and page make-up all by Veloce on Apple Mac.
Printed by Replika Press in India.

Introduction & thanks
– the purpose of this book

There are lots of books about the Triumph Bonneville, about its history, performance, lineage and the minutiae of its specification, but none of them tell you what to look for when buying one secondhand. That's what this book is about – a straightforward, practical guide to buying a used Bonnie. It won't list all the correct colour combinations for each year, or analyse the bike's design philosophy, or consider its background as part of a troubled industry – there are excellent books listed at the end of this one which do all of that. But hopefully it *will* help you avoid buying a dud.

Over 29 years of production, the Bonneville is for some the definitive postwar British vertical twin, perhaps even the definitive British bike of all time, with all its strengths, weaknesses and character. Although there might seem to be a wide range of models and special editions, all are based around the same 649cc or 747cc vertical twin. There were plenty of changes over the years, but none of them changed the basic format of this classic British bike.

1964 T120 Bonneville.

The Bonnie is special, not just because of its character as a lusty A and B road bike, but because it was a survivor. It was launched in 1959, as a latecomer to the range, and named in honour of the 214mph speed record set by a very special Triumph at Bonneville Salt Flats, Utah, three years earlier. The name stuck, and the Bonnie became the flagship of the Meriden factory, riding Triumph's '60s boom as thousands of bikes were exported to the USA. Yet

Special edition Silver Jubilee Bonneville.

Early Bonnie, a 1961 pre-unit 650.

it also survived the hard times of the '70s, carrying on after the rest of the British motorcycle industry had fallen by the wayside. As the sole product of the Meriden workers' co-operative, it holds a special place in biking history, and was even briefly revived in the mid-1980s by spares specialist LF Harris.

Aside from all the history, the Bonneville remains a tremendous classic to own, so long as you're prepared to look after it, and the last Bonnies truly deserve the term 'practical classic'. Whichever one you choose, it should be fast, agile and good looking, and on a twisty English B road, there's nothing like a Bonnie.

Thanks to all those people who helped, and without whom this book would not have happened. Triumph restorer Hugh Brown (The Bike Shed – 01920 830931) gave me lots of useful tips, and Kevin Wall at Forest Classics (01725 514422) was also a great help. Special thanks are due to Roger Fogg and Howard Stevens, who brought together a whole gaggle of Bonnevilles for me to photograph. And to the owners: Richard Marsh, Mark Venton, Adrian Salisbury, Adam Mason, David Smith, Gerald Sedgemore, Richard Crook, Peter Nichols and Howard Stevens. Also to James Robinson of *The Classic Motorcycle* and Nigel Clark at *Old Bike Mart*.

Essential Buyer's Guide™ currency
At the time of publication a BG unit of currency "●" equals approximately £1.00/US$2.00/Euro 1.50. Please adjust to suit current exchange rates.

Contents

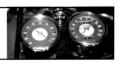

www.velocebooks.com / www.veloce.co.uk
All current books • New book news • Special offers • Gift vouchers

1 Is it the right bike for you?

– marriage guidance

Tall and short riders
Compared to modern bikes, Bonnevilles are relatively small and light, especially by 650/750 standards. But short riders should steer clear of the 1971 bikes, with their sky scraping 34.5in seat height.

Running costs
Surprisingly modest. Even ridden fairly hard, Bonnevilles will return 45-55mpg, and the single-carb equivalents are better still. Old Triumphs are not gas guzzlers.

Maintenance
Make no mistake, any bike from this era needs more TLC and sympathy than modern machines. You'll need to change the oil every 1500 miles to maximise engine life, and just keep an eye open for things coming loose or going out of adjustment. Not a 'ride it, forget it' sort of bike.

Kick-starting
Very few Bonnies had an electric start (some of the early 1980s bikes did have). In any case, a well set up Triumph will not be hard to start, though it has to be said that kick-starting is more about technique than strength.

Usability
If you need to do lots of motorway (freeway) miles, or urban commuting, then a Bonnie is not the bike for you. They are, however, easy and very satisfying to ride on an open, twisty road.

Parts availability
Excellent, probably better than for any other classic bike, with many parts still being made (you won't be able to build a new Bonneville from new parts, though).

Parts costs
Very good. Because so many Bonnies were made and are still around (and some parts didn't change for years), spares aren't expensive.

Insurance group
Go for a classic bike limited mileage policy, such as that offered by Carole Nash or Footman James in the UK, and you won't pay much.

Investment potential
Depends on the bike. A lot of the investment potential of a Bonneville depends on when it was made. Pre-unit (1959-62) bikes are rare and will always keep their value, and pre-oil-in-frame 650s are expensive but unlikely to lose value. Later (1970s) bikes are the most affordable, but unlikely to see big increases – lots have survived and they don't have the same classic caché as the earlier machines. Rarities like the TSS, TSX or Executive should fare better.

Foibles
Triumph twins vibrate and leak oil – that's part of motorcycling folklore. However, most riders aren't bothered by the vibes, which only really intrude at high revs, and a well assembled engine in good condition shouldn't leak.

Plus points
One of the cult motorcycles of all time, with good looks and torquey, punchy performance. Lightweight, too, if you're used to big, porky modern bikes.

Minus points
Like any motorcycle of this era, the Bonneville needs looking after (though that can be part of the attraction) and the pre-'71s are expensive, certainly if you just want some weekend fun.

Alternatives
First and foremost, the single-carb equivalent Triumphs, the Trophies and Tigers, which are almost as fast as a Bonnie but easier to live with. If you want a British twin, there are loads of alternatives from Norton, BSA, AJS, Matchless, et al.

Nice '67 T120 in US specification.

2 Cost considerations
– affordable, or a money pit?

Triumph spares, by and large, are not expensive. T140 parts, in particular, seem good value compared with spares for modern Japanese bikes. It's labour costs that mount up, rather than parts. If you are prepared to service the bike yourself, a Bonneville should be quite affordable to run (at 45-55mpg, it's even quite good on fuel).

Complete restoration (basket case to concours) around ●x10,000
Air cleaner element (T140) ●x8
Alternator (Lucas RM21, complete) ●x150
Brake shoes (7in rear) ●x27
Brake shoes (8in tls front) ●x25
Brake pads ●x10.50
Brake disc ●x38
Battery (12v Lucas) ●x20
Camshafts ●x85 each
Carburettor (Amal Concentric 900) ●x98
Clutch assy complete (T140) ●x227
Clutch centre (T120) ●x105
Cylinder barrel (T140) ●x155
Downpipes (with balance pipe) ●x110 pair

Electronic ignition ●x85
Fork stanchions (T120) ●x68 pair
Fork stanchions (T140) ●x55 pair
Fuel tank (T140, US, primer) ●x225
Gasket set from ●x30
Gearbox mainshaft ●x155
Headlamp (glass/reflector only) ●x30
Headlamp (complete, T140) ●x100
Mudguard (front) ●x55
Mudguard (rear) ●x225
Oil pump (Morgo) ●x80
Rear chain (Renolds) ●x45
Pistons (Hepolite, T120) ●x125 pair
Primary chain ●x40
Rear shocks ●x101 pair
Seat (complete) ●x110
Silencers (Toga, T120) ●x168 pair
Silencers (Toga, T140) ●x130 pair
Speedometer head ('68-'78) ●x65
Tank badge (T140) ●x42.50 pair
Valve guides ●x8 each
Wiring loom (T120) ●x45
Wiring loom (T140) ●x65

Most parts necessary to keep a Bonnie on the road are easy to find.

If parts are missing, new or secondhand replacements should be available.

Parts prices for T140s, in particular, are very reasonable.

3 Living with a Bonneville
– will you get along together?

Let's get one thing clear right away. A Bonneville is not the bike for 21st century commuting. While Belstaff-clad young bloods did just that in the 1960s, they were keen enough to take on the intensive maintenance that went with it (or happy to live with the oil leaks and unreliability that resulted from neglect). In an age where bikes need only an oil check and chain tweak between major services, the Bonneville demands a lot more looking after. We live in an age when consumer products keep working without much attention – old bikes aren't like that.

Having said all that, the later the model, then generally the easier it is to live with, and some folk still do use later machines as everyday transport. However, for most, the Bonnie is a second or third bike, kept in the garage for good days. Even then, it demands a different mindset to that involved in riding a modern bike. The relationship is based on constant awareness of how the bike is running: has that nut vibrated loose? Is that the beginning of a leak from the rocker box? If an indicator ceases to function, is it the bulb or just a loose connector? All these little things are part of Bonneville ownership, but many owners would say they are part of what makes owning one (or indeed most old bikes) more satisfying than a new machine. You develop a relationship with it that is quite different to that had with a bike that always starts on the button and never goes wrong.

Bonnies, like all old bikes, need plenty of TLC.

Later T140s are easier to live with.

Pre-unit Bonnevilles are undoubtedly the most demanding. They've got plenty of performance, but don't have the brakes to match (worth bearing in mind for 21st century traffic conditions). The pre-1961 carburettor setup (with a remote reservoir feeding the float chambers) is tricky to prime, and offers lumpy low speed running. Adjusting the primary chain involves moving the gearbox in the frame. 6-volt magneto electrics can be upgraded to 12-volt, but the pre-unit Bonnie is best reserved for sunny days on twisty roads.

The same is really true of the 1963-70 unit 650, though steady improvement throughout its life means that the later the bike, the easier it is to live with. Some argue that later 1960s Bonnies were over-tuned, in an effort to keep up with horsepower demand from the USA, and the encroaching Japanese competition. But this is really outweighed by the practical advances: 12-volt electrics, better brakes and lubrication, a stiffer, better-handling frame and more thorough breathing to combat oil leaks. All of these things make the later '60s Bonnevilles less demanding than the earlier ones. They also had those high compression pistons and peakier E3134 cams for both inlet and exhaust, which boosted power over 5000rpm but also increased vibration and made the engine less happy at low speeds. Be realistic about the sort of riding you want to do. If it really is just sunny day blasts, then none

An early '60s Bonnie is a beautiful thing on a sunny day.

of this will matter, but for more relaxed riding, a more softly-tuned engine will be a happier companion.

Of course, there's nothing to stop an owner fitting lower compression pistons and kindlier cams, and it all really depends on how serious you are about originality. A better choice might be to look for a milder single-carb Trophy 650, and leave the Bonneville alone.

All of the hot tuning was Triumph's attempt to keep up with much younger bikes from Japan, but when the Bonnie became a 750 in 1973, its character changed. Don't be put off by the larger capacity; the first T140 was little heavier than the T120, physically no bigger, and had a lower seat than the '71 650s. Just as important, Triumph had finally accepted that its venerable twin couldn't keep up with the Japanese fours, and detuned it with milder cams and lower compression. The result was more low- and mid-range torque than the highly strung 650, and better flexibility at low speed. A Bonneville 750 isn't as blood and thunder as its predecessors, but it is more

1970 T120; thought by some to be the ultimate Bonneville.

relaxed – which is best for you depends what you want out of the riding experience.

As with the earlier Bonnevilles, steady improvements were made over the years, such as electronic ignition, timing-side roller bearing, and high-output alternator in 1979, and a four-valve oil pump the following year. These are all good, pragmatic changes that make the Bonnie easier to run day-to-day, and, of course, as the bikes didn't change fundamentally, it's possible to apply them retrospectively to older machines. Purists might protest about originality, but many of these improvements don't affect the bike's appearance at all. Once again, it's all down to what sort of riding you're intending to do, how happy you are with fettling, and whether you're a stickler for complete originality.

The eight-valve TSS promised to combine the traditional Bonneville feel with a lot more performance, and it certainly had the latter, though its production life was too short to overcome the teething troubles of slipping liners, porous castings, and rapidly wearing cams. Even now, the final performance Bonnie is more of a challenge to own than the standard T140.

A Bonneville can be made very easy to live with, especially if you're prepared to sacrifice a little unseen originality. But whatever you do, it's not a 'push button and ride' sort of bike.

The 1982 TSS was one of the very last in production.

See Chapter 12 for value assessment. This chapter shows, in relative percentage terms, the value of individual models in good condition. There were many variations on the Bonneville theme over its long production life, and this chapter also looks at the strengths and weaknesses of each model, so that you can decide which is best for you. Basically, the Bonnie's evolution can be divided into six stages.

Range availability
1959-62 Pre-unit 650s – T120
1970-70 Unit 650s – T120
1974-74 Oil-in-frame 650s – T120, T120R, T120RV
1977-77 Early Meriden 750s – T140V
1978-83 Late Meriden 750s – T140E, TSS, TSX
1988-88 Harris 750s
Single-carb Triumphs
Thruxton/TT

1959-62 pre-unit 650s
The original Bonneville was launched for 1959 in response to demand from the rapidly growing US market for more power, plus the influence of Production Racing at home. It was based on the existing T110, with the same frame and 649cc vertical twin, but with a number of significant changes. Twin carburettors were fitted – which always set the Bonnie apart from other big Triumph twins – with remote rubber-mounted float chambers. There were high-lift cams (E3134 inlet and E3352 exhaust), a higher 8.5:1 compression ratio, and a forged, one-piece crankshaft, plus a Lucas competition magneto. It all added up to 46bhp at 6500rpm and a 108mph top speed. There was a new duplex (twin downtube) frame for 1960, and the T110 headlamp nacelle and touring handlebars were ditched in favour of a separate chrome shell headlamp and flatter bars.
Strengths/weaknesses: The original,

Early pre-unit Bonnevilles are rare and sought-after.

These first T120s deliver a 'raw' riding experience.

raw Bonneville experience, with rip-roaring performance. Weak brakes and tricky to set up carbs (pre-1961) and electrics not as reliable as the later 12-volt alternator system.
230%

1963-70 unit 650s

Perhaps the definitive Bonneville, and certainly the best seller – they were exported to the USA in their thousands, and 250,000 Bonnies in total are said to have been built up to 1972. Unit construction Bonnevilles have the engine and gearbox built in one piece – they were cheaper to make, could use an alternator, and had a cleaner appearance than the pre-unit. The bike featured a new, nine-stud head, to prevent cracking, and the single downtube frame was stiffer and handled better than the last of the pre-units. More chassis changes (a different steering head angle,

Early unit construction bike, still with 6-volt electrics.

1966 brought many worthwhile changes, including 12-volt electrics and better handling.

1970 T120 was the last of the old-style Bonnevilles.

and better swingarm support from 1966) turned the unit 650 Bonneville into the best handling bike of its time. Other worthwhile improvements that year were 12-volt electrics, better lubrication, a bigger oil tank, and a new front brake with 44 per cent more shoe area. An 8in twin leading shoe front brake and two-way damped forks followed in '68. Many enthusiasts regard the 1969-70 Bonnevilles, which featured a breather system and other changes to tackle oil leaks, as the ultimate Bonnies.

Strengths/weaknesses: Better frame, electrics, and brakes, especially from 1966, make the unit 650 Bonnevilles particularly attractive. Still fast, but with more refinement than the pre-unit machines. However, ever increasing demands for power also brought more vibration.
200%

1971-74 oil-in-frame 650s

This was the least-loved Bonneville, though also rare in the UK, as many were exported. The model was unveiled for 1971 and launched as part of a major update to the entire range, with an all-new frame, forks and (big step, this) flashing indicators. It proved to be a disaster, however – the new frame, using its large top tube as an oil tank, was prone to fractures, allowed the engine to run hot, and forced a massive seat height of 34.5in. The new conical hub drum brakes were poor, and the bikes' skimpy mudguards and exposed fork stanchions were clearly aimed at West Coast USA rather than damp UK. However, the oil-in-frame 650s did settle down after a while. The frame,

Least-loved Bonnie – this is a '72 model – and often the cheapest to buy.

for all its faults, handled well, and from mid-1972 the seat was lowered to a more practical 31.5in. That year also brought an optional five-speed gearbox (making the bike a T120V), interchangeable with the old cluster, and 1973 saw more substantial mudguards and a front disc brake. There were few changes the following year, when production ceased due to the Meriden blockade.

Strengths/weaknesses: The early oil-in-frame Bonnevilles certainly had their weaknesses, and some still consider them to be an inferior bike. However, they do have a certain style, and most of the frame's teething troubles were ironed out by 1973, with the worthwhile addition of that disc brake.
75%

1973-78 Meriden T140s

The T140, the 750cc Bonneville, was built at Meriden for 10 years. It's the most numerous and most affordable Bonnie of all. Launched in 1973, it reflected the increasing popularity of the 750 sector of the market. It was no faster than the 650, and, in fact, top end power was slightly down – to allow the venerable twin to cope with its bigger capacity, Triumph detuned it, with lower compression and milder cams. The result was a flexible, torquey machine, though vibration was worse. It also had a

Special editions like this Silver Jubilee can fetch high prices.

ten-stud cylinder-head. Like the 650, it came in US and UK configurations, and from mid-1975 changed to a left-foot gearchange (dictated by US regulations) along with a rear disc brake and easier-to-use switchgear. In 1977, the Silver Jubilee Bonneville was the first of several special editions, finished in silver plus patriotic red, white and blue. That one is better for collecting than riding, as the special paint and chrome don't last well.

Strengths/weaknesses: Different in character to the 650 Bonneville, the 750 is more of a tourer than a sports bike, but it's still a torquey and pleasant machine to ride, despite the vibration. Still hot running, thanks to the oil-bearing frame, but also the cheapest route to Bonneville ownership. 60%

1979-83 Meriden T140s

The final Meriden-built Bonnies are often referred to as practical classics, and with good reason – they developed over the years into well-sorted bikes that give enjoyable, trouble-free riding. No one pretended that the Bonnie was a performance bike any more, and now it was more about the riding experience than sheer performance.

New for 1979 was the T140E, with a new cylinder-head allowing parallel inlet tracts for its Amal Mk2 Concentric carburettors. Designed to meet US emissions regulations, it did away with the infamous tickler buttons, and returned 50-55mpg. The crank was

more thoroughly machined to reduce vibration, and gained an SKF roller bearing on the timing side. Lucas Rita electronic ignition was another big step forward, for a more accurate spark that didn't slip out of time, as was a high-output, three-phase alternator, and clearer switchgear.

The 1979 T140D Special was a factory custom, in gold and black with alloy wheels, and was followed in 1980 by the Executive, complete with hard luggage and a cockpit fairing. Another option that year was electric start (Bonnies thus equipped came with a gold 'Electro' badge on the side panels) which, once past its teething troubles, worked quite well. A new, four-valve oil pump featured on all 1980 Bonnies. There was another special edition in 1981, the Royal Wedding Bonnie, in US or UK form, with chrome tank, black engine cases, alloy wheels and twin front discs.

There was big news the following year, with the TSS touted as the new performance Triumph. Its eight-valve, high-compression twin claimed 57bhp, and it could crack 120mph, but the bike proved troublesome in production, with porous cylinder-heads, blowing head gaskets and rapidly wearing cams all featuring. More straightforward was the TSX factory custom, with high bars, a low-slung look and fat rear tyre, plus short, stubby megaphone silencers. More developments were planned for '83, including the AV anti-vibration frame, but production ceased at the end of 1982.

Strengths/weaknesses: The T140E is a good choice for regular use. It's a little down on power compared with early 750 Bonnies, but is smoother and more refined plus better on fuel. Meriden's quality control improved at this time, though like any Triumph twin, the T140E does need a sympathetic owner. About half the final Bonnevilles were fitted with electric start, and 25 years on, the teething troubles should have been sorted. Well kept special editions should keep their value, but the troublesome and very rare TSS is more of a challenge to own.
100%

1986-88 Harris Bonnevilles

In 1986, the long-awaited Harris Triumph Bonneville was launched. Triumph spares manufacturer LF Harris of Newton Abbot bought the rights to make Bonnies from John Bloor, who now owned the name. With many of the original components unavailable, Harris fitted Paioli forks, Brembo brakes, Lanfranconi silencers, Radaelli wheel rims and Magura switchgear. The Harris Bonnies were offered in basic kick-start form only, and there were reports of patchy quality, though contemporary tests thought they felt more taut than the Meriden machines. They also had more ground clearance, an improved oil filter, updated fuse box, and stainless steel mudguards. An estimated 1260 Harris Bonnevilles were built in just over two years.

Strengths/weaknesses: Not favoured by the collectors, for their high Italian parts content, the Harris Bonnevilles did incorporate some worthwhile improvements. Otherwise, they were very similar to the T140s made at Meriden, and the same comments apply.
100%

Trophy/Tiger – the milder Bonneville

Alongside the twin-carb Bonneville, throughout its long production run, Triumph offered a single-carb equivalent: the pre-unit Tiger 110, the 1960s Trophy 650, and the 1970s Tiger 650 and 750. All the same comments apply as for the twin-carb Bonneville, as each was updated alongside the Bonnie in just the same way. None has the magic of the Bonneville name, but the single-carb version of Triumph's big twin is more flexible than the Bonnie, easier to set up, less thirsty, and not that much slower in the real world. In fact, late 1960s Trophies were really single-carb

Bonnevilles, with the same cams and pistons. For 1960s single-carb 650s, deduct around 20 per cent from the equivalent Bonneville price. Later single carbs are priced the same as the Bonnie.

US or UK spec?

Later Bonnevilles are usually referred to as being in US- or UK-spec, a reflection of the vital importance of the North American market to Triumph. There are few differences, the main ones being the style of fuel tank and bars – US-spec Bonnies came with high bars and a pretty, slimline 2.5 or 3 gallon fuel tank; UK bikes had a slab-sided 4-gallon tank and lower bars. Both styles were

Slimmer, smaller tank on US-spec bikes.

Silver Jubilee shows bigger tank and lower bars of UK-spec T140s.

offered in Britain from 1973, though, of course, many US-spec bikes have since been re-imported. Which is best is in the eye of the beholder, and whether you prefer a laid back or slightly lean forward riding position. The US bikes are arguably prettier; the UK ones have a longer tank range.

Competition specials

Triumph twins were highly competitive in the 1960s, for both road racing and off-road, though there were only two factory specials, built specifically for competition, during that time. The Thruxton Bonneville was launched in 1964, fitted with all the options needed to go Production Class racing, though it was road legal. Some of these engine and chassis improvements later appeared on standard Bonnevilles. The Thruxton was listed for a mere six months, and it's thought that less than 70 were made.

If the Thruxton Bonneville was aimed at British racers, the TT120C TT Special was for their US counterparts. Sold in high-compression form, without silencers, the TT was intended for dirt competition riding only, and was not road legal. It was listed from 1964-67, only in the North American market.

Both Thruxton and TT Specials command high prices when offered for sale. Buyers should beware of fakes – easily done with the bolt-on

Very rare T120TT, with straight-through pipes and no lights.

parts – and documentary proof of the bike's history is essential.

5 Before you view
– be well informed

To avoid a wasted journey, and the disappointment of finding that the bike does not match your expectations, it will help if you're very clear about what questions you want to ask before you pick up the phone. Some of these points might appear basic, but when you're excited about the prospect of buying your dream classic, it's amazing how some of the most obvious things slip the mind ... Also, check the current values of the model you're after in the classified ads of the classic bike magazines.

Where is the bike?
Is it going to be worth travelling to the next county/state, or even across a border? A locally-advertised machine, although it may not sound very interesting, can add to your knowledge for very little effort, so make a visit – it might even be in better condition than you expect.

Dealer or private sale?
Establish early on if the bike is being sold by its owner or by a trader. A private owner should have all the history, so don't be afraid to ask detailed questions. A dealer may have more limited knowledge of the bike's history, but should have some documentation. A dealer may offer a warranty/guarantee (ask for a printed copy).

Cost of collection and delivery?
A dealer may well be used to quoting for delivery. A private owner may agree to meet you halfway, but only agree to this after you've seen the bike at the vendor's address to validate the documents. Conversely, you could meet halfway and agree the sale, but insist on meeting at the vendor's address for the handover.

View – when and where?
It's always preferable to view at the vendor's home or business premises. In the case of a private sale, the bike's documentation should tally with the vendor's name and address. Arrange to view only in daylight, and avoid a wet day – the vendor may be reluctant to let you take a test ride if it's wet.

Reason for sale?
Do make this one of the first questions. Why is the bike being sold and how long has it been with the current owner? How many previous owners?

Condition?
Ask for an honest appraisal of the bike's condition. Ask specifically about some of the check items described in Chapter 9.

All original specification?
A completely original Bonnie will be worth more than a modified one, but certain mods (later oil pump, electronic ignition) can also indicate a conscientious owner who has been actively riding/caring for the machine.

Matching data/legal ownership?

Do frame, engine numbers and licence plate match the official registration document? Is the owner's name and address recorded in the official registration documents?

For those countries that require an annual test of roadworthiness, does the bike have a document showing it complies (an MoT certificate in the UK, which can be verified on 0845 600 5977)?

If it's a 1973 or later Bonneville, does it carry a current road fund licence/license plate tag? Earlier bikes are road tax exempt in the UK.

Does the vendor own the bike outright? Money might be owed to a finance company or bank: the bike could even be stolen. Several organisations will supply data on ownership, based on the bike's licence plate number, for a fee. Such companies can often also tell you whether the bike has been 'written off' by an insurance company. In the UK these organisations can supply vehicle data:

HPI – 01722 422 422 – www.hpicheck.com
AA – 0870 600 0836 – www.theaa.com
RAC – 0870 533 3660 – www.rac.co.uk
Other countries will have similar organisations.

Unleaded fuel?

Has the bike been modified to run on unleaded fuel?

Insurance?

Check with your existing insurer before setting out – your current policy might not cover you if you do buy the bike and decide to ride it home.

How you can pay

A cheque/check will take several days to clear and the seller may prefer to sell to a cash buyer. However, a banker's draft (a cheque issued by a bank) is as good as cash, but safer, so contact your own bank and become familiar with the formalities that are necessary to obtain one.

Buying at auction?

If the intention is to buy at auction see Chapter 10 for further advice.

Professional vehicle check (mechanical examination)

There are often marque/model specialists who will undertake professional examination of a vehicle on your behalf. Owners clubs may be able to put you in touch with such specialists.

6 Inspection equipment

– these items will really help

This book
Reading glasses (if you need them for close work)
Overalls
Digital camera
Compression tester
A friend, preferably a knowledgeable enthusiast

Before you rush out of the door, gather together a few items that will help as you work your way around the bike. This book is designed to be your guide at every step, so take it along and use the check boxes in Chapter 9 to help you assess each area of the bike. Don't be afraid to let the seller see you using it.

Take your reading glasses, if you need them, to read documents and make close up inspections.

Be prepared to get dirty. Take along a pair of overalls, if you have them.

If you have the use of a digital camera, take it along so that later you can study some areas of the bike more closely. Take a picture of any part of the bike that causes you concern, and seek a friend's opinion.

A compression tester is easy to use. It screws into the sparkplug holes, and on a Bonneville these couldn't be easier to get to. With the ignition off, turn the engine over on full throttle to get the compression reading.

Ideally, have a friend or knowledgeable enthusiast accompany you: a second opinion is always valuable.

Spotting a fake

However good the condition of the bike, however well it's been restored, there's not much point in going any further if it's pretending to be something it isn't. Although it's seen as an iconic model in its own right, the Bonnie's spec differed only in a few ways from its milder, single-carb equivalents, the Trophy 650 and Tiger 650/750, which are often worth less. It's a relatively simple job for the unscrupulous to fit a twin-carb Bonneville head to a basic Triumph and hope that no one notices the difference.

The answer lies in the engine number, stamped on the left-hand side, just below the cylinder barrel. 'T120' or 'T140' indicates that it's a genuine Bonnie, though numbers can be tampered with. Later machines had this area stamped with the Triumph logo, to make tampering more difficult.

Now look for the frame number, on the left-hand side of the downtube. This should carry the same number as the engine. If it doesn't, the bike has had

Frame number is located by the headstock.

a different engine fitted at some point. There may have been a good reason for this, but not having matching engine/frame numbers reduces the bike's value. Beware of standard Bonnies dressed up as the ultra-rare and sought-after Thruxton Bonneville or T120C TT. Check the engine/frame numbers with records held by the VMCC or the owners club.

Finding non-matching numbers doesn't necessarily mean it's time to walk away. The bike itself may still be an honest machine with plenty to offer – you just need to make it clear to the seller that you know it isn't 100 per cent original (or isn't a real Bonnie) and start negotiating on price.

Documentation

If the seller claims to be the bike's owner, make sure he/she really is by checking the registration document, which, in the UK, is the V5C. The person listed on the V5 isn't necessarily the legal owner, but the details should match those of whoever is selling the bike. Also use the V5C to check the engine/frame numbers.

An annual roadworthiness certificate – the 'MoT' in the UK – is handy proof that the bike was roadworthy when tested. A whole sheaf of them gives evidence of the bike's history – when it was actively being used, and what the mileage was. The more of these come with the bike, the better.

General condition

Put the bike on its centre stand, to shed equal light on both sides, and take a good, slow walk around it. If it's claimed to be restored, and has a nice shiny tank and engine cases, look more closely – how far does the 'restored' finish go? Are

Take a general look around the bike in good light.

the nooks and crannies behind the gearbox as spotless as the fuel tank? If not, the bike may have been given a quick smarten up to sell. A generally faded look all over isn't necessarily a bad thing – it suggests a machine that hasn't been restored, and isn't trying to pretend that it has.

Look at the engine – by far the most expensive and time consuming thing to put right if anything's wrong. A lot of people will have told you that all old Triumphs leak oil, but there shouldn't be any serious leaks if the engine is in good condition and has been put together well. It shouldn't be spattered with lube, or have oily drips underneath. Even if it's dry on top, get down on your knees and have a peek at the underside of the crankcase – nice and dry, or covered in oil?

The engine number (on the left-hand side below the cylinder barrel) should match the frame number.

Take the bike off the centre stand and start the engine – it should fire up within two or three kicks, and rev up crisply and cleanly without showing blue or black smoke. Some top end clatter is normal, but listen for rumbles and knocks from the bottom end, and clonks from the primary drive – any of these are indications of serious work being required. While the engine's running, check that the ignition light or ammeter show that the electrics are charging, and that the oil light (on T140s) goes out.

Switch the engine off and put the bike back on its centre stand. Check for play in the forks, headstock and swingarm. Are there leaks from the front forks or rear shocks? Are details like the seat, badges and tank colour right for the year of the bike? (A little research helps here, and the reference books listed at the end of this volume have all this information.)

Don't be fooled by the glitter – take a closer look.

Are nuts/bolt heads chewed up or rounded-off? Is there damage to the casings around the bolt heads? Has someone attacked the fixings with a hammer and chisel? All these are sure signs of a careless previous owner with more enthusiasm than skill, coupled with a dash of impatience. Not a good sign.

Do the engine and frame numbers match? It's not the end of the world if they don't, but an engine/frame that didn't leave Meriden together will reduce the value of the bike, however good its condition.

The frame number is at the top of the frame downtube, on the left-hand side.

Minor oil leaks aren't a problem (though they are a bargaining point), but serious ones suggest correspondingly serious mechanical wear, or neglect.

Listen to the engine running. Clonks or rumbles from the primary drive may indicate wear in the clutch and its shock absorber, the engine sprocket chattering on worn splines, or a loose alternator rotor.

9 Serious evaluation

– 30 minutes for years of enjoyment

Circle the Excellent, Good, Average or Poor box of each section as you go along. The totting up procedure is detailed at the end of the chapter. Be realistic in your marking!

Engine/frame numbers

Ex | Gd | Av | Po

[4] [3] [2] [1]

A golden rule to buying a secondhand Bonneville – if you want a genuine, original bike, that is – is to check that the engine and frame numbers are the same. If they match, then that engine and frame were bolted together on the Meriden production line, and have stayed together ever since. That's why so many classified ads state 'matching engine/frame numbers' – it's a good selling point.

The golden rule – check the engine and frame numbers.

If they don't match, you may still have a perfectly good, functioning motorcycle, and there may be a perfectly good reason for mismatching numbers, such as a replacement engine. But the engine and frame are likely to be from different years, and the engine may not be a genuine Bonneville unit. That's no great disaster if you're not that bothered about complete originality, but it should be reflected in the price, and the bike will be more difficult to sell later.

Later engine numbers have an embossed background to prevent tampering.

The engine number is located on the left-hand side, just below the cylinder barrel joint; the frame number is also on the left, at the top of the downtube by the steering head – it's sometimes

The frame number is difficult to read, but it is there.

Check that the crankcase numbers match.

tricky to decipher, especially if the frame has been repainted or powder coated, but it is there. 'T120' in the engine/frame number denotes a Bonneville 650, 'T140' is a 750 – anything else is not a genuine Bonnie. Later bikes had the engine number background stamped with the Triumph logo, to make it more difficult to tamper with.

Now get down on the ground (it's why you brought the overalls). Triumph crankcases come in two halves – right and left. Right at the base of the crankcase, on one of the bolt bosses, you should find two numbers, one on each crankcase half. If these match, then the two halves left the factory together. For an explanation of which engine/frame numbers relate to which year, see Chapter 17.

Paint

Ex Gd Av Po
4 3 2 1

Triumphs have always been good looking bikes, and the paintwork makes a big contribution. The good news is that there's not that much of it, just tank, sidepanels and mudguards – many later 750s had chromed rather than painted mudguards, with plain black sidepanels, making a repaint easier still. Having said that, don't underestimate the cost of a professional job, which is well worth having done, as the fuel tank, in particular, is such a focal point of the whole bike. Look for evidence of quick and cheap resprays, with pinstriping, for example, that doesn't line up with the tank badges. Light staining around the filler cap, from spilt fuel, might polish out,

Crazing like this needs a respray to put right.

but could also require a respray. Generally speaking, faded original paintwork isn't necessarily a bad thing, and, in fact, some riders prefer this unrestored look – there are so many restored Bonnevilles around, that an honest-looking original, even if a little faded around the edges, has its own appeal.

Most Bonnevilles had some sort of two-tone colour scheme, and for originality it's important to get the right one for the year of the bike, along with its correct pinstriping. The reference books give a complete listing. Paint availability shouldn't be a problem, as there are often modern equivalents – Triumph Pacific Blue from the 1960s, for example (used on the Bonneville for 1965), is the same as a Ford metallic blue.

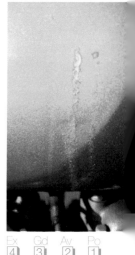

Blisters can't be polished out!

Chrome

Ex Gd Av Po
4 3 2 1

Chrome-plating is another big visual plus on the Bonneville, used on the silencers, headlamp shell, handlebars, parcel grid, mirrors, some mudguards, tank badges and other parts. The quality of Meriden's original plating is generally pretty good, though we are talking 30 or 40 years on now, so don't expect it to be pristine.

The Harris Bonnevilles of 1986-88 are less well thought of, some of the

Chromed gearbox and primary drive covers on the Silver Jubilee don't hold up well.

Minor rust spots on a silencer could indicate serious rot inside.

chrome deteriorating quite early on in life. Another model to watch for is the Silver Jubilee Bonneville, the silver, red white and blue special edition offered in 1977 to commemorate the Queen's first 25 years on the throne. As well as the special paintwork, Silver Jubilee Bonnies had chrome-plated primary drive cover, timing gear cover, and gearbox cover. These looked lovely in the official pictures, but the chrome didn't always take well to the alloy casings, and doesn't weather well either. It's also less efficient at dispersing heat than the plain alloy, always an issue for the oil-in-frame Triumphs.

Whichever Bonnie you're looking at, check the chrome for rust, pitting, and general dullness. Minor blemishes can be polished away, but otherwise you're looking at a replating bill. If the silencers are seriously rotted, it's a better idea to budget for a new pair – less hassle than getting the old ones replated.

Tinwork

Ex   Gd   Av   Po
4   3   2   1

In one respect, buying a secondhand bike is far easier than purchasing a used car – there's far less bodywork to worry about. This is particularly true of the Bonneville, which only has tank, mudguards and sidepanels. Even in the early 1960s, when Triumph was fitting the 'bathtub' rear enclosure to its touring/commuter twins, the Bonnie was left naked. And only the very first T120s of 1959 featured Triumph's headlamp nacelle, which gives a smooth appearance in conjunction with the fully shrouded forks. It only lasted a year, though, as a separate chrome headlight shell was thought more appropriate to Triumph's sporting flagship. If looking at a '59 Bonnie, check that the nacelle is true, and free of

Nice paintwork, but look out for 'wonky' tank trim.

Mudguards should be straight and rust-free.

If originality is important, check that colour and pinstriping is correct for the year.

Oil tank should be dent- and leak-free.

dents and rust, but the first-year Bonneville is such a collector's item that this instant recognition factor should be in good condition.

Mudguards, too, should be straight, free of rust around the rims, and securely bolted to the bike. The front mudguard stays varied in detail over the years: substantial twin stays through the 1960s; spindly rubber-mounted stays for '71/72; and a return to the stronger type from '73. The Harris Bonnie front mudguards were bolted to the fork legs only.

Up to 1970, the sidepanels were rounded black items, the right-hand one acting as an oil tank, and the matching left-hand one housing the toolkit. The oil tank should be checked for leaks through the seams, as repair entails removal and flushing out before it can be put right. From 1971 on, the sidepanels were flat (still in plain black), and covers only, as the oil tank was now part of the frame. Until 1978, these panels came in two pieces – don't expect them to line up precisely!

The fuel tank should be checked for leaks around the tap and along the seams, as well as for dents and rust. Watch out for patches of filler. As with the early oil tank, repairing leaks means flushing out the tank (which has to be thorough – you don't want any fuel vapour hanging about when the welding torch is fired up), but the fuel tank is at least easy to remove. Pinhole leaks can often be cured by Petseal, but anything more serious needs a proper repair. If the tank is beyond saving, new ones, in both US and UK style, are available, though once it's been painted, that's not a cheap option. So a very poor condition tank is a good bargaining lever.

Trim

Ex Gd Av Po
4 3 2 1

Bonnevilles were not fitted with over-elaborate trim, and on T140s this usually consists of just the tank and sidepanel badges. The Silver Jubilee, T140D Special and Royal Wedding special editions, plus the TSS, all had their own sidepanel badges, and these may become hard to find in the future.

Tank badges come in various styles, according to year: the grille-style badge up to 1965; the 'eyebrow' in '66-68; and the less elaborate 'picture frame' badge from '69. UK-spec T140s always had a simple 'Triumph' script, while the US-spec bikes retained the '69-on one until 1979, when they, too, adopted the simple script. Whatever the badge, it should be fixed firmly in place,

The infamous parcel grid – a must for every '60s Triumph.

26

with unpitted chrome and flake-free paint. All these tank badges are available new.

T120 Bonnevilles had more trim on the fuel tank, notably a chrome strip down the centre to hide the upper seam. They also had the infamous parcel grid, designed to allow the rider to carry small items on top of the tank. Triumph stopped fitting this traditional item in 1969, after a celebrated (if that's the right word) case in which an American rider sued the company after being emasculated by his Triumph's parcel grid during a collision. So, originality or (for male riders) personal safety – the choice is yours. If it's there, the grid should be securely mounted, with chrome in good condition.

Ex	Gd	Av	Po
4	3	2	1

Seat

All Bonnevilles had a dual seat which neatly hinged up to reveal (depending on year) the battery, toolkit and oil filler. There was a wide range of styles, and, once again, if originality is important, you'll need to have the right one. The earliest pre-unit bikes had a thin, plain black seat, while the move to unit construction in 1963 brought a two-tone seat with grey top and lower trim, plus black sides. Beware of oily fingers smudging the light grey finish. A ribbed, all-black seat with a chrome strip around the base arrived for 1968, thinned down for 1972 as part of the attempt to reduce the '71 Bonnie's excessive seat height. It was restyled over the years, while the Silver Jubilee had its own version with red piping. Buy a 1979 UK-spec T140E, and the seat comes in a sort of autumnal brown – original, but not pretty. By the this time, the ribbing had given way to cross hatching, though the TSS and TSX went back to a plain ribbed finish.

A grabstrap was optional on some

T120s, with a proper grabrail fitted from 1969 (initially optional).

Whichever seat a Bonneville has, the points to look for are the same. The metal pan can rust, which will eventually give way, though this is easy to check. Covers can split, which, of course, allows rain in, which the foam padding soaks up ... and never dries out. That's a recipe for a permanently wet backside, or a rock hard seat on frosty mornings (the author speaks from experience). New covers and complete seats in various styles are available, though recovering an old seat is a specialist job.

Rubbers

Ex	Gd	Av	Po
4	3	2	1

Worn footrest rubbers are a good sign of high mileage, though as they're so cheap and easy to replace, not an infallible one. They should be secure on the footrest and free of splits or tears. If the footrest itself is bent upwards, that's a sure sign

Footrest and gearlever rubbers must be secure and undamaged.

the bike has been down the road at some point, so look for other telltale signs on that side. The kick-start and gearchange rubbers are also easy to replace, so well worn ones could indicate owner neglect. On kick-start bikes, beware the worn smooth rubber – your foot's liable to slip off while kicking the bike over, with painful results as the lever slams back into your leg. The rubber should also be firm on the lever and not drop off after half a dozen kicks. Of course, if the engine needs that many kicks to fire it up, then something's wrong there anyway.

Wear like this indicates high mileage.

Frame

Ex	Gd	Av	Po
4	3	2	1

There were four basic types of Bonneville frame. The first single downtube frame lasted only a year, superseded in 1960 by a duplex type, which gave better handling. The duplex frame was stiffened further for '61 by the addition of an extra tube, though this had the side-effect of increasing vibration. Unit construction

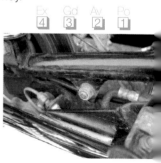

Poor frame paintwork like this really needs a strip down and stove enamelling to put right.

in 1963 saw a return to a single downtube frame with a well-braced swingarm support. Changes to this frame for 1966 turned all Triumph 650s (not just the Bonnie) into some of the best handling bikes of their time. Finally, all-new for 1971 was the oil-in-frame design, carrying engine oil in the large top tube. Early examples had troubles with fractures and oil leaks, but soon settled down – all '71-on Bonnevilles used this frame.

A frame that is really shabby necessitates a strip down and repaint, though, as with the other paintwork, if it's original and fits with the patina of the bike, then there's a good case for leaving it as it is.

How a restored frame can look.

Look for bent brackets, which can be heated and bent back into shape, and cracks around them, which can be welded. Those for horn and exhaust pipes are usually the first to succumb to vibration.

The most important job is to check whether the main frame is straight and true. Crash damage may have bent it, putting the wheels out of line. One way of checking is by an experienced eye, string and a straight edge, but the surest way to ascertain a frame's straightness is on the test ride – any serious misalignment should be obvious in the way the bike handles.

Stands

Ex Gd Av Po
4   3   2   1

All Bonnevilles were fitted with both centre- and side-stands, though some owners removed the centre-stand to improve cornering clearance – an issue that especially affected the T140 on the left-hand side. If the stand's still in place, scrape marks indicate a history of hard riding (not that this is a problem; the Bonnie is an agile bike that encourages spirited riding, and scraped stands do not necessarily equal lunatic owners).

1963-67 side-stands had weak frame clamps.

Otherwise, Triumph stands are strong and secure.

Both stands should be secure, of course, but especially watch 1963-67 side-stands – the mounting clamp doesn't reach right around the frame tube, and this is a weak point. When on the centre-stand, the bike shouldn't wobble or lean, a sign of serious stand wear and/or imminent collapse. This affects bikes which have been started and left idling on the centre-stand – all the vibration is transmitted to ground via the stand, which doesn't do it much good.

Lights

Ex ☐4 Gd ☐3 Av ☐2 Po ☐1

Triumph electrics improved dramatically with a 12-volt system in 1966, and a high-output alternator in '79. Later bikes also had halogen headlight bulbs, though the bulb will have probably been replaced several times by now. Whatever the age, look for a tarnished or rusted reflector, which in the UK is an MoT failure, though reflectors, bulbs, glass and headlight shells are all available.

Headlight reflector can corrode (this one's fine).

Rear light style varied over the years.

There were three main styles of rear light: 1959-70; '71/72; and the big squared-off item fitted from 1973 to the end of production. All are widely available as pattern parts, though one handy modification that doesn't alter the outward appearance in any way is an LED rear/stop light bulb. This is a straight swap for the standard bulb, but won't blow, leaving you taillight-less on a dark night.

Electrics/wiring

Ex ☐4 Gd ☐3 Av ☐2 Po ☐1

A traditional bête noire of Triumph twins, though the electrical system was updated over the years. The dynamo was swapped for an alternator in 1960, while retaining magneto ignition, which was dropped for 1963 with the arrival of unit construction, replaced by twin contact breaker points in the timing cover. Twelve volts replaced six in 1966, with the addition of a zenor diode (the finned item hiding beneath the headlight) to control charging from 1968. Another

All bullet connectors should be clean and tight.

The alternator is generally reliable.

Water can enter the rear brake light switch.

useful improvement in '68 was the fitting of Lucas 6CA contact breakers, which allowed independent adjustment of the spark for each cylinder, and thus more accurate timing. However, the real solution to electrical problems is electronic ignition. Meriden fitted that from 1979, along with a beefier, three-phase alternator. Both of these were big steps forward, the latter boosting charge at low revs and allowing daytime headlight running.

Check that the zenor diode is securely mounted, and with good connections.

Regardless of which system is present, the electrical system still needs checking. A good general indication of the owner's attitude is the condition of the wiring – is it tidy and neat, or flopping around? The many bullet connectors need to be clean and tight, and many odd electrical problems are simply down to bad connections or a poor earth. Up to 1970, Bonnevilles came with an ammeter, which at least gives some indication that all is well in the charging circuit. Early 'ignition' warning lights are there simply to inform you that the ignition is on, not whether the alternator is doing its job.

Finally, check that everything works: lights, horn, indicators (fitted post '71, but often removed by owners) and stop light (water can enter the rear brake switch).

Wheels/tyres

All Bonnevilles used spoked wheels with chromed steel rims, apart from the T140D Special, Royal Wedding Special and TSX, which had seven-spoke alloys. On the steel wheels, check the chrome condition on the rims – rechroming entails a complete dismantle and rebuild of the wheel. Check that none of the spokes are loose, and give each one a gentle tap with a screwdriver – any that are 'off key' will need retensioning. Alloy wheels should be checked for cracks, though there's no evidence that they are prone to them.

Ex Gd Av Po
4   3   2   1

Tyres aren't expensive, but worn ones are a good bargaining point.

Check for loose or bent spokes.

Tyres should be to at least the legal minimum. That's at least 1mm of tread depth across at least three-quarters of the breadth of the tyre. Or if the tread doesn't reach that far across the breadth (true of some modern tyres) then any tread showing must be at least 1mm deep. Beware of bikes that have been left standing (especially on the side-stand) for some time, allowing the tyres to crack and deteriorate – it's no reason to reject the bike, but it's a good bargaining tool. New tyres in Bonneville sizes are widely available.

Wheel bearings

Ex | Gd | Av | Po
4 | 3 | 2 | 1

Wheel bearings aren't expensive, but fitting them is a hassle, and if there's play, it could affect the handling. To check them, put the bike on its centre-stand, put the steering on full lock, and try rocking the front wheel in a vertical plane, then spin the wheel and listen for signs of roughness. Do the same for the rear wheel.

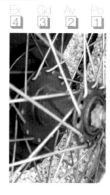

Worn rear wheel bearings show up in play at the wheel rim.

It's the same story at the front.

Steering head bearings

Ex | Gd | Av | Po
4 | 3 | 2 | 1

Again, the bearings don't cost and arm or leg, but trouble here can affect the handling, and changing them is a big job. With the bike on the centre-stand, swing the handlebars from lock to lock. They should move freely, with no hint of roughness or stiff patches – if there are any signs of wear in the bearings, budget for replacements. To check for play, put the steering on full lock, grip the front wheel, and try rocking it back and forth.

Swingarm bearings

Ex | Gd | Av | Po
4 | 3 | 2 | 1

These are essential for good handling. They should have been regularly greased – if they haven't, rapid wear, or even seizure, can result, the latter if the bike has been left standing for some time. To check for wear, get hold of the rear end of the arm on one side and try rocking the complete swingarm from side-to-side. There should be no perceptible movement.

Worn swingarm bearings upset the handling, and replacing them is a big job.

Suspension

All Bonnevilles used the same basic suspension setup: front telescopic forks and twin rear dampers, which were later adjustable. The forks were fully shrouded on the very first Bonnies, and partially shrouded with rubber gaiters from 1962. From '71, to go with the new oil-bearing frame, Ceriani type forks with exposed stanchions were fitted. These did a good job, but suffered from exposure to British weather, and gaiters were reintroduced on UK-spec Bonnies in 1973 – US machines (also offered in Britain, confusingly enough) stuck with the sexier exposed forks.

Exposed fork stanchions wear more quickly than gaitered ones.

Shocks should be leak-free and firm.

Replacement shocks are readily available.

Check forks for play and oil leaks.

The rear shocks lost their shrouding in 1969, and then stayed that way, with chrome springs, until the very end. The very last bikes, including the TSS, used Marzocchi Strada units, with pre-load adjustment and remote reservoir.

Check the forks and rear shocks for leaks. The fork stanchion's chrome-plate eventually pits, especially when exposed to the elements and/or the bike has been used in winter. When that happens, it rapidly destroys the oil seals – hence the leaks. New stanchions, or reground and replated existing ones, are the answer, as there's little point in fitting new seals to rough forks.

Check for play by grabbing the bottom of the forks and trying to rock them back and forth; play here indicates worn bushes. Worn out rear shocks will manifest themselves as a weave over 70mph, and sick forks will likewise spoil the handling.

Instruments

Bonneville instruments are exactly what you'd expect from a British bike: speedometer and rev counter, plus an ammeter in the '60s. Very early machines had the rev counter as an option (though most bikes will have been fitted with one by now). There were various styles, depending on year, but Triumph instruments didn't change as frequently as the rest of the bike, with grey-faced matching Smiths speedo and rev counter replaced by black-faced ones in 1971 (when the ammeter was dropped) and finally by French-made Veglia units.

Typical '60s T120 instrument set.

Final style of Smiths or Veglia instruments, with centrally-mounted warning lights.

Checking the speedo works obviously has to wait for the test ride – if nothing is working, the cable is the most likely culprit, but if either mileometer or speedo have ceased to function, while the other is still working, then there's something wrong internally – instrument repair is best left to a specialist. A battered and bent chrome bezel suggests that a previous owner has tried to effect a repair.

Only very early Bonnevilles did without a rev counter – note the ammeter in the headlight shell.

Engine/gearbox – general impression

You can tell a lot about the likely condition of a Triumph twin without hearing it run. These engines are easy to work on, and the drawback of that is that it encourages keen and/or impecunious owners to take things apart themselves, often without the proper tools. Look for 'chewed up' screw or Allen bolt heads, and rounded off bolts, plus damage to the casings surrounding them.

It's part of motorcycling folklore that old Triumphs leak oil, but this isn't necessarily the case. As long as the engine is in good condition and has been properly put together, it should be reasonably oil tight, certainly in the case of the later 750s. Some light misting isn't a bad sign, but if the bike has a puddle of oil underneath it, and the engine/gearbox is covered in lubricant, then walk away – unless, of course, the price reflects the condition. An engine like that is likely to need a complete rebuild.

A well put together, cared-for Bonneville twin should look like this.

Triumph engines will carry on running when in very poor condition. One professional restorer I know of was given a unit to rebuild. He found that a previous owner had chrome-plated the crank journals and cam bearings, which had subsequently broken up. One conrod was cracked, and three of the pushrods were bent. It was also a 'bitsa' engine, made up of random parts: a '64 bottom end with a '71 cylinder head,

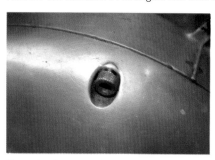

Have the fasteners (and their surroundings) been attacked with a hammer and chisel?

Not concours, but running well and perfectly serviceable.

A thin oil mist isn't necessarily a problem. Can you spot the welded repair in the head?

Triumphs don't *have* to leak oil – check around this area after your test ride.

one 'R' spec cam follower, and three standard ones. In the UK, that engine cost £4000 to rebuild.

Many of the same comments apply to the gearbox – look for chewed fasteners and signs of neglect. Remove the oil filler cap and stick a finger inside to check whether the oil had been changed recently – nice clean EP90 ... or a frothy sludge.

Engine – starting/idling

Triumph engines are good starters, and one in good condition should fire up within two or three kicks. If it doesn't, there's something wrong. The most likely culprit (if electronic ignition hasn't been fitted) is simply maladjusted contact breaker points and ignition timing. A more serious cause is poor compression, which indicates general wear and will need a top end rebuild to rectify. Take a compression tester along, and use it.

Electric start Bonnevilles had their teething troubles, but these should have been overcome by now, and the starter should engage cleanly without excessive noise. About half the

Ex	Gd	Av	Po
4	3	2	1

1981-82 Bonnies were fitted with push-button starting, so there are still a few around.

Once started, the engine should idle evenly on both cylinders.

The Triumph engine needs a hefty kick, but should start readily.

If electric start is fitted, try it.

If it sounds and feels lumpy and uneven, then contact breaker or carburettor adjustments are the most likely cause, but a knowledgeable owner should already have these spot-on. If either carburettor is worn, both new parts and complete carbs are available. Even when in excellent condition, the Bonnie's twin Amals do need to be kept synchronised, and one answer is to opt for a single-carb Tiger instead, or (if you're not worried about originality) convert the Bonnie to single-carb spec. Another possible cause of uneven idling and running is damage to the hoses connecting the carburettors to air filters and inlet stubs – these can cause air leaks and upset the mixture.

Engine – smoke/noise

If you're used to quiet, smooth, modern, water-cooled motorcycles, don't be alarmed by the merry clattering emanating from the Triumph's rocker boxes, as they all do that. Even among old British bikes, the Triumph twin had a reputation for mechanical noise from the top end. Adjusting the tappets is an easy enough job, though access is far better on the '73-on bikes, with their full-width rocker box covers.

A sign of real trouble is knocking or rumbling from the bottom end, which will mean a complete engine rebuild for sure. Whether it's big-ends or mains that need attention, the cure is engine out and a complete strip to find out what's wrong. Beware of impressively loud megaphone silencers that may mask the more subtle knockings of a sick bottom end. Don't buy a bike that's making these noises, unless it's cheap. Engine parts to cure all of these problems are widely available, for both 650 and 750 Bonnies.

This much blue smoke indicates a top end rebuild on the horizon.

Listen for rumbling from the primary drive.

Look back at the silencers and blip the throttle. Blue smoke means the engine is burning oil and is a sign of general wear in the top end. That means a rebore (again, parts, including oversize pistons, are available) but inevitably other problems will come up once the engine is apart – the valves and guides will probably need replacing as well. Black smoke, indicating rich running, is less of a problem, caused by carburettor wear or (fingers crossed) simply a blocked air filter. Bikes without air filters should be avoided, as you don't know what nasties the motor has ingested. Early Bonnevilles left the factory without filters, but refusing to fit them in the 21st century is really taking originality too far.

Seriously blued pipes are a sign of overheating – this much is fine.

Expect some clatter from the top end – they all do that.

Primary drive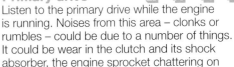

Listen to the primary drive while the engine is running. Noises from this area – clonks or rumbles – could be due to a number of things. It could be wear in the clutch and its shock absorber, the engine sprocket chattering on worn splines, or the alternator rotor coming loose on the crank's driving shaft. Of course, you won't know which without taking the primary drive cover off, but if the seller acknowledges that a noise is there, it's another good lever to reduce the price.

Primary chains on pre-unit Bonnevilles (1959-62) are prone to rapid wear, thanks to less effective lubrication. In theory, the unit construction bikes' primary chain, running in its nice clean oil bath, should have a much longer life, but this still needs to be checked. Adjustment of the chain tensioner, through the drain plug hole, is messy and awkward (though easier with the proper tool) and may have been neglected.

Noises in the primary drive indicate clutch or alternator trouble.

A loose alternator, clutch, or slack primary chain will be the cause.

Chain/sprockets

With the engine switched off, examine the final drive chain and sprockets. Is the chain clean, well lubed and properly adjusted? The best way to check how worn it is is to take hold of a link and try to pull it rearwards away from the sprocket. It should only reveal a small portion of the sprocket teeth – any more, and it needs replacing.

Check the rear sprocket teeth for

Sprockets are readily available, and not expensive.

Worn sprockets mean a new chain as well.

wear – if they have a hooked appearance, the sprocket needs replacing. Ditto, if any teeth are damaged or missing. And if the rear sprocket needs replacing, then the gearbox sprocket will too. Chain and sprockets aren't massively expensive, but changing the gearbox sprocket takes time.

Battery

Hinge up the seat and check the battery (or in the case of early 12-volt bikes, the twin 6-volt batteries). Acid splashes indicate overcharging. The correct electrolyte level is a good sign of a meticulous owner, and do check that the battery is securely kept in place by its rubber strap. If it isn't, the battery can leap upwards over bumps and short out against the metal seat base. (Again, author's experience).

Check that the battery is secure, and well-filled with electrolyte.

Engine/gearbox mountings

These need to be completely solid, with no missing or loose bolts (which would mean that the bike would be unrideable). The exact design changed over the years (some mountings were welded to the frame, some bolted) but the points to check are the same.

Engine/gearbox mounts are welded or bolted to the frame – all should be solid.

Exhaust

Most Bonnies left the factory with twin silencers, though some have since been fitted with aftermarket two-into-one systems. These save a little weight and make chain adjustment (both primary and rear) easier. From 1969, all bikes had a balance pipe between the downpipes.

Check that the downpipes are secure in the cylinder head (looseness causes air leaks), and examine all joints for looseness and leaks, all of which are MoT failures. The silencers should be secure, firmly mounted, and in solid condition. Replacements for the various types are all available. Toga is the main aftermarket supplier.

A balance pipe was fitted to late T120s and all T140s with 2-into-2 systems.

Bonnevilles don't have to be loud if the silencers are sound.

Replacement silencers are easy to find.

Test ride

Ex 4 Gd 3 Av 2 Po 1

The test ride should last at least 15 minutes, and you should be doing the riding – not the seller riding with you on the pillion. It's understandable that some sellers are reluctant to let a complete stranger loose on their pride and joy, but it does go with the territory of selling a bike, and as long as you leave an article of faith (usually the vehicle you arrived in) then a test ride is a reasonable request. Take your driving licence in case the seller wants to see it.

Main warning lights

Ex 4 Gd 3 Av 2 Po 1

All Bonnies have an ignition warning light, but on T120s this only serves to tell you that the ignition is on – it doesn't warn of poor charging, which is what the ammeter is for. Don't expect the ammeter to give a foolproof reading at high revs, but so long as it shows a positive charge with the lights on at moderate revs, all is well. T140s had a conventional ignition light, which should flicker out once revs are over idling speed.

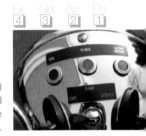

Oil light (fitted to T140s) should flicker out above idling speed.

Ditto the oil pressure warning light – T120s didn't have one of these.

T120 and early T140 warning lights are mounted in the headlight shell. From 1979, they moved to a separate cluster between the speedometer and rev counter. These later Bonnies also have a neutral light, though it's not infallible, and most riders still find neutral by feel.

Ammeter on T120s is in place of an ignition low-charge warning light.

Engine performance

Ex 4 Gd 3 Av 2 Po 1

A Bonneville in good condition – whether 650 or 750 – should give good, beefy acceleration in the mid-range. Even the highly-tuned T120s have a decent amount of torque, and all bikes should pull cleanly. And despite all the talk of vibration, all Bonnies should be smooth and free-revving up to 5000rpm. A Bonneville should not feel flat, lazy and lifeless.

Check for hesitation, which shouldn't happen – a Bonnie with well set-up ignition and carburetion will pull crisp and clean. Spitting back through the carbs can be caused by a lack of air filters. Although seen by one and all as a sports machine (especially the T120), the Bonneville should be quite tractable at low speeds, especially the T140.

If possible, cruise the bike at 70mph for five minutes, then check for oil leaks – there shouldn't be anything more than a slight misting. The maximum comfortable

Ready for the road ... a good Bonnie should give strong performance.

Triumph's twin should pull hard and cleanly if all is well.

cruising speed is around 75mph, partly down to the riding position on T140s (especially those with US-spec high bars) but also because vibration becomes intrusive over 5000rpm. All Bonnevilles will crack 100mph, but they weren't designed for the motorway age (even if some were made then), so it's unfair to expect them to keep up with modern motorway speeds without ill effects for both machine and rider.

Clutch operation

The clutch is heavier than on many modern bikes, but take up should be smooth and positive. Nor should it drag or slip, despite the tales of all Triumph clutches dragging. To check this, select first gear from a standstill. A small crunch is normal, but a full-blooded graunch, followed by a leap forward, means the clutch is dragging. However, the cure is usually down to careful adjustment rather than the wholesale replacement of parts.

Clutch will be heavyish, but shouldn't be stiff or jerky, or slip or drag.

Gearbox operation

Triumph gearboxes – in both 4-speed T120s and 5-speed T140s – work well, with a clean, positive shift. Watch for stiffness, notchiness and whining. They're also reliable, and, given regular oil changes, should not give trouble.

Don't expect foolproof neutral at a standstill, but gear changes should be positive.

Difficulty in finding neutral at a standstill is not inevitable, so long as the clutch has been set up correctly, so reluctance here is no reason to suspect the bike, though it's often easier to slip into neutral just as you roll to a standstill. However, false neutrals, or slipping out of gear, are sure signs of trouble.

Handling

Triumph's reputation for making good handling bikes, especially from the mid-1960s onwards, was well deserved, and the same holds true today, though bear in mind that early Bonnies, especially the 1959-62 pre-unit, are not as surefooted at high speeds as the later machines.

Bonnevilles are relatively light bikes with stiff suspension, easy to flick through corners, and highly agile. Any vagueness and weaving is usually down to worn forks, rear shocks, or tyres – it's not inherent. They should never feel soft and wallowy – if they do, the suspension condition is the first thing to recheck. Early T140s suffered from a lack of ground clearance on the left-hand side (the centre-stand being the culprit) though this should only worry hard riders.

Brakes

Ex   Gd   Av   Po
[4]   [3]   [2]   [1]

What to expect here really depends on what era Bonneville you're looking at. The pre-1966 bikes' 8in front and 7in rear drums weren't really up to the demands of a 100mph+ machine, especially in the case of pre-'62 bikes. Factor in modern traffic conditions, and you need to bear the brakes in mind, and not expect modern disc performance on the test ride.

Things improved dramatically from 1966, with a 44 per cent increase in front

This rear disc has lost most of its chrome plating.

1971-73 twin-leading shoe conical hub drum doesn't have a good reputation.

Front disc brake was a great improvement.

Late 1960s twin-leading shoe front drum is well respected, and a popular upgrade for earlier bikes.

brake lining area. These brakes do match the performance, especially the twin leading-shoe front drum from 1968, and they should be smooth and progressive. The 'conical hub' drums fitted in 1971/72 are less well thought of, and 'spongey' in operation.

A front disc appeared in 1973, the rear following in '77. The discs were chrome-plated, which can chew up pads and dramatically shorten their life as the chrome deteriorates. Modern sintered pads are not recommended with the chrome, as they destroy the plating. If the chrome is still there, it's a good idea to have this skimmed off, which avoids all of these problems. On the test ride, check that both disc brakes work well without feeling soft or spongey.

Cables

All the control cables – brakes, throttle and choke – should work smoothly without stiffness or jerking. Poorly lubricated, badly adjusted cables are an indication of general neglect, and the same goes for badly routed cables.

Check brake/ clutch/speedo cables are undamaged and well routed.

Switchgear

Switchgear changed enormously over the Bonneville's production run. Early machines were simple in the extreme, with a rotary light switch, plus cut-out and horn buttons on the handlebars. The lighting switch later became a toggle in the headlight shell, and the 1971 new generation sported new Lucas alloy switches (confusingly unlabelled at first). Updated Lucas switches arrived for 1977, and the final Bonnies used Magura switchgear.

Whatever is fitted, check that it works positively and reliably – early Lucas alloy switches could let water in, with inevitable results. Malfunctioning switches are usually a simple problem to solve, but another reason to bargain over price.

Final switchgear was simple but effective.

1971-73 Lucas switches are unlabelled, and vulnerable to water ingress.

Air lever (choke) should work smoothly.

Evaluation procedure

Add up the points scored –

136 = first class, possibly concours; 102 = good/very good; 68 = average; 34 = poor.

Bikes scoring over 95 should be completely useable and require the minimum of repair, although continued maintenance and care will be required. Bikes scoring between 34 and 69 will require a full restoration – the cost of which will be much the same regardless of score. Bikes scoring between 69 and 94 will need very careful assessment of the repair/restoration costs so as to gain a realistic purchase value.

10 Auctions
– sold! Another way to buy your dream

Auction pros & cons

Pros: Prices will usually be lower than those of dealers or private sellers, and you might bag a real bargain on the day. Auctioneers have usually established clear title with the seller. At the venue you can usually examine documentation relating to the bike.

Cons: You have to rely on a sketchy catalogue description of condition and history. The opportunity to inspect is limited, and you cannot ride the bike. Auction machines can be a little below par and may require some work. It's easy to overbid. There will usually be a buyer's premium to pay in addition to the auction price.

Which auction?

Auctions by established auctioneers are advertised in motorcycle magazines and on the auction houses' websites. A catalogue, or a simple printed list of the lots for auction, might only be available a day or two ahead, though often lots are listed and pictured on auctioneers' websites much earlier. Contact the auction company to ask if previous auction selling prices are available, as this is useful information (details of past sales are often available on websites).

Catalogue, entry fee and payment details

When you purchase the catalogue of the bikes in the auction, it often acts as a ticket for two people to attend the viewing days and the auction. Catalogue details tend to be comparatively brief, but will include information such as 'one owner from new, low mileage, full service history', etc. It will also usually show a guide price to give you some idea of what to expect to pay, and will tell you what is charged as a 'buyer's premium'. The catalogue will also contain details of acceptable forms of payment. At the fall of the hammer an immediate deposit is usually required, with the balance payable within 24 hours. If the plan is to pay by cash there may be a cash limit. Some auctions will accept payment by debit card. Sometimes credit or charge cards are acceptable, but will often incur an extra charge. A bank draft or bank transfer will have to be arranged in advance with your own bank as well as with the auction house. No bike will be released before all payments are cleared. If delays occur in payment transfers then storage costs can accrue.

Buyer's premium

A buyer's premium will be added to the hammer price: don't forget this in your calculations. It's not usual for there to be a further state tax or local tax on the purchase price and/or on the buyer's premium.

Viewing

In some instances it's possible to view on the day, or days before, as well as in the hours prior to the auction. There are auction officials available who are willing to help out if need be. While the officials may start the engine for you, a test ride is out of the question. Crawling under and around the bike as much as you want is permitted. You can also ask to see any available documentation.

Bidding

Before you take part in the auction, decide your maximum bid – and stick to it! It may take a while for the auctioneer to reach the lot you're interested in, so use that time to observe how other bidders behave. When it's the turn of your bike, attract the auctioneer's attention and make an early bid. The auctioneer will then look to you for a reaction every time another bid is made, usually the bids will be in fixed increments until the bidding slows, when smaller increments will often be accepted before the hammer falls. If you want to withdraw from the bidding, make sure the auctioneer understands your intentions – a vigorous shake of the head when he or she looks to you for the next bid should do the trick!

Assuming that you are the successful bidder, the auctioneer will note your card or paddle number, and from that moment on you will be responsible for the bike.

If it's unsold, either because it failed to reach the reserve or because there was little interest, it may be possible to negotiate with the owner, via the auctioneers, after the sale is over.

Successful bid

There are two more items to think about. How to get the bike home, and insurance. If you can't ride it, your own or a hired trailer is one way, another is to have it shipped using the facilities of a local company. The auction house will also have details of companies specialising in the transport of bikes.

Insurance for immediate cover can usually be purchased on site, but it may be more cost-effective to make arrangements with your own insurance company in advance, and then call to confirm the full details.

eBay & other online auctions

eBay and other online auctions could land you a Bonneville at a bargain price, though you'd be foolhardy to bid without examining it first, something most vendors encourage. A useful feature of eBay is that the geographical location of the bike is shown, so you can narrow your choices to those within a realistic radius of home. Be prepared to be outbid in the last few moments of the auction. Remember, your bid is binding and that it will be very, very difficult to get restitution in the case of a crooked vendor fleecing you – caveat emptor!

Be aware that some bikes offered for sale in online auctions are 'ghost' machines. Don't part with any cash without being sure that the vehicle does actually exist and is as described (usually, pre-bidding inspection is possible).

Auctioneers

Bonhams www.bonhams.com
British Car Auctions BCA) www.bca-europe.com or www.british-car-auctions.co.uk
Cheffins www.cheffins.co.uk
eBay www.ebay.com
H&H www.classic-auctions.co.uk
Palmer Snell www.palmersnell.co.uk
Shannons www.shannons.com.au
Silver www.silverauctions.com

11 Paperwork
– correct documentation is essential!

The paper trail
Classic bikes sometimes come with a large portfolio of paperwork accumulated and passed on by a succession of proud owners. This documentation represents the real history of the machine, from which you can deduce how well it's been cared for, how much it's been used, which specialists have worked on it, and the dates of major repairs and restorations. All of this will be priceless to you as the new owner, so be very wary of bikes with little paperwork to support their claimed history.

Registration documents
All countries/states have some form of registration for private vehicles, whether it's like the American 'pink slip' system or the British 'log book' system.
It is essential to check that the registration document is genuine, that it relates to the bike in question, and that all the details are correctly recorded, including frame and engine numbers (if these are shown). If you are buying from the previous owner, his or her name and address will be recorded in the document: this will not be the case if you are buying from a dealer.

In the UK the current (Euro-aligned) registration document is the V5C, and is printed in coloured sections of blue, green and pink. The blue section relates to the motorcycle specification, the green section has details of the registered keeper (who is not necessarily the legal owner), and the pink section is sent to the DVLA in the UK when the bike is sold. A small section in yellow deals with selling within the motor trade.

In the UK the DVLA will provide details of earlier keepers of the bike upon payment of a small fee, and much can be learned in this way.

If the bike has a foreign registration there may be expensive and time-consuming formalities to complete: do you really want the hassle? More recently, many of the thousands of Bonnevilles exported to the USA have been re-imported to the UK. It sounds like a great chance to buy a Triumph that has only been used on dry, West Coast roads, with the added glamour of US heritage. Plus the fact that US prices tend to be lower – a good condition late '60s T120 will sell for around ●x2500, which is little more than half the UK price.

However, you'll have to buy the bike sight unseen, and the paperwork involved in importing and re-registering is a daunting prospect. It means employing a shipping agent and budgetting-in the shipping costs. Then there's (at the time of writing) 6 per cent import duty on the bike and shipping costs, and 17.5 per cent VAT on the whole lot. Unless you're after a rare US-only spec bike, it may not be worth it.

Roadworthiness certificate
Most country/state administrations require that bikes are regularly tested to prove that they are safe to use on the public highway. In the UK that test (the MoT) is carried out at approved testing stations, for a fee. In the USA the requirement varies, but most states insist on an emissions test every two years as a minimum, while the police are charged with pulling over unsafe-looking vehicles.

In the UK the test is required on an annual basis once a vehicle becomes three years old. Of particular relevance for older bikes is that the certificate issued includes the mileage reading recorded at the test date and, therefore, becomes an independent record of that machine's history. Ask the seller if previous certificates are available. Without an MoT the vehicle should be trailered to its new home, unless you insist that a valid MoT is part of the deal (not such a bad idea this, as at least you will know the bike was roadworthy on the day it was tested and you don't need to wait for the old certificate to expire before having the test done.)

Road licence

The administration of every country/state charges some kind of tax for the use of its road system, the actual form of the 'road licence' and how it is displayed varying enormously country to country and state to state.

Whatever the form of the road licence, it must relate to the vehicle carrying it, and must be present and valid if the bike is to be ridden on the public highway legally. The value of the licence will depend on the length of time it will continue to be valid.

In the UK if a bike is untaxed because it has not been used for a period of time, the owner has to inform the licencing authorities, otherwise the vehicle's date-related registration number will be lost and there will be a painful amount of paperwork to get it re-registered. Also in the UK, bikes built before the end of 1972 are exempt from road tax, but they must still display a valid disc. Bike clubs can often provide formal proof that a particular machine qualifies for this valuable concession.

Certificates of authenticity

For many makes of classic bike, it is possible to get a certificate proving the age and authenticity (e.g. engine and frame numbers, paint colour and trim) of a particular machine. These are sometimes called 'Heritage Certificates' and if the bike comes with one of these it is a definite bonus. If you want to obtain one, the owners club is the best starting point.

Valuation certificate

Hopefully, the vendor will have a recent valuation certificate, or letter signed by a recognised expert stating how much he, or she, believes the particular bike to be worth (such documents, together with photos, are usually needed to get 'agreed value' insurance). Generally, such documents should act only as confirmation of your own assessment of the bike rather than a guarantee of value as the expert has probably not seen it in the flesh. The easiest way to find out how to obtain a formal valuation is to contact the owners club.

Service history

Often these bikes will have been serviced at home by enthusiastic (and hopefully capable) owners for a good number of years. Nevertheless, try to obtain as much service history and other paperwork pertaining to the bike as you can. Naturally, specialist garage receipts score most points in the value stakes. However, anything helps in the great authenticity game, items like the original bill of sale, handbook, parts invoices and repair bills, adding to the story and the character of the machine. Even a brochure correct to the year of the bike's manufacture is a useful document and something that you could well have to search hard to locate in future years. If the seller claims that the bike has been restored, then expect receipts and other evidence from a specialist restorer.

If the seller claims to have carried out regular servicing, ask what work was completed, when, and seek some evidence of it being carried out. Your assessment of the bike's overall condition should tell you whether the seller's claims are genuine.

Restoration photographs

If the seller tells you that the bike has been restored, then expect to be shown a series of photographs taken while the restoration was under way. Pictures taken at various stages, and from various angles, should help you gauge the thoroughness of the work. If you buy the bike, ask if you can have all the photographs as they form an important part of its history. It's surprising how many sellers are happy to part with their bike and accept your cash, but want to hang on to their photographs! In the latter event, you may be able to persuade the vendor to get a set of copies made.

12 What's it worth to you?

– let your head rule your heart!

Condition

If the bike you've been looking at is really ratty, then you've probably not bothered to use the marking system in Chapter 9 – 30 minute evaluation. You may not have even got as far as using that chapter at all!

If you did use the marking system you'll know whether the bike is in Excellent (maybe Concours), Good, Average or Poor condition or, perhaps, somewhere in between these categories.

To keep up to date with prices, buy the latest editions of the classic bike magazines and check the classified and dealer ads – these are particularly useful as they enable you to compare private and dealer prices. Most of the magazines run auction reports as well, which publish the actual selling prices, as do auction house websites.

Values have been fairly stable for some time, but some models will always be more sought-after than others. For example, it's clear that the rare 1959 pre-unit Bonnevilles command the highest prices of all, but if you want an all-round practical classic, then that's not the bike for you. Prices can go down as well as up, but the '59 Bonnie will probably remain the most sought-after.

Bear in mind that a bike that is truly a recent show winner could be worth more than the highest price usually seen. Assuming that the bike you have in mind is not in show/concours condition, then relate the level of condition that you judge it to be in with the appropriate price in the adverts. How does the figure compare with the asking price? Before you start haggling with the seller, consider what affect any variation from standard specification might have on the bike's value. This is a personal thing: for some, absolute originality is non-negotiable; while others see non-standard parts as an opportunity to pick up a bargain. Do your research in the reference books, so that you know the bike's spec when it left the factory. That way, you shouldn't end up paying a top-dollar original price for a non-original bike.

If you are buying from a dealer, remember there will be a dealer's premium on the price.

Striking a deal

Negotiate on the basis of your condition assessment, mileage, and fault rectification cost. Also take into account the bike's specification. Be realistic about the value, but don't be completely intractable: a small compromise on the part of the vendor or buyer will often facilitate a deal at little real cost.

There's a romance about restoration projects, about bringing a sick bike back into blooming health, and it's tempting to buy something that 'just needs a few small jobs' to bring it up to scratch. But there are two things to think about: one, once you've got the bike home and start taking it apart, those few small jobs could turn into big ones; two, restoration takes time, which is a precious thing in itself. Be honest with yourself – will you get as much pleasure from working on the bike as you will from riding it?

Of course, you could hand the whole lot over to a professional, and the biggest cost involved there is not the new parts, but the sheer labour involved. Such restorations don't come cheap, and, if taking this route, there are three other issues to bear in mind as well.

First, make it absolutely clear what you want doing. Do you want the bike to be 100 per cent original at the end of the process, or simply usable? Do you want a concours finish, or are you prepared to put up with a few blemishes on the original parts?

Secondly, make sure that not only is a detailed estimate involved, but that it is more-or-less binding. There are too many stories of a person quoted one figure only to be presented with an invoice for a far larger one!

Ripe for restoration ... but do you want the hassle?

Third, check that the company you're dealing with has a good reputation – the owners club, or one of the reputable parts suppliers, should be able to make a few recommendations.

Restoring a Bonnie yourself requires a number of skills, which is fine if you already have them, but if you haven't it's good not to make your newly acquired bike part of the learning curve! Can you weld? Are you confident about building up an engine? Do you have a warm, well-lit garage with a solid workbench and good selection of tools?

Restored bikes can end up better than new, but it'll cost.

Be prepared for a top-notch professional to put you on a lengthy waiting list or, if tackling a restoration yourself, expect things to go wrong and set aside extra time to complete the task. Restorations can stretch into years when things like life intrude,

A full restoration to this standard could cost ●x10,000.

A ground-up rebuild like this takes time.

Chewed up crankcase from Hugh Brown's black museum.

so it's good to have some sort of target date.

A rolling restoration is tempting, especially as the summers start to pass with your bike still off the road. This is not the way to achieve a concours finish, which can only really be achieved via a thorough nut-and-bolt rebuild, without the bike getting wet, gritty and salty in the meantime. But there's a lot to be said for a rolling restoration. Riding it helps keep your interest up as the bike's condition improves, and it's also more affordable than trying to do everything in one go. In the long run, it will take longer, but you'll get some on-road fun out of the bike in the meantime.

14 Paint problems
– bad complexion, including dimples, pimples and bubbles

Paint faults generally occur due to lack of protection/maintenance, or to poor preparation prior to a respray or touch-up. Some of the following conditions may be present in the bike you're looking at:

Orange peel
This appears as an uneven paint surface, similar to the appearance of the skin of an orange. The fault is caused by the failure of atomised paint droplets to flow into each other when they hit

Repainting tank badges isn't a big job.

the surface. It's sometimes possible to rub out the effect with proprietary paint cutting/rubbing compound or very fine grades of abrasive paper. A respray may be necessary in severe cases. Consult a paint shop for advice.

Cracking
Severe cases are likely to have been caused by too heavy an application of paint (or filler beneath the paint). Also, insufficient stirring of the paint before application can lead to the components being improperly mixed, and cracking can result. Incompatibility with the paint already on the panel can have a similar effect. To rectify, it's necessary to rub down to a smooth, sound finish before respraying the problem area.

Crazing
Sometimes the paint takes on a crazed rather than a cracked appearance when the problems mentioned under 'cracking' are present. This problem can also be caused

by a reaction between the underlying surface and the paint. Paint removal and respraying the problem area is usually the only solution.

Blistering
Almost always caused by corrosion of the metal beneath the paint. Usually

Crazing, a subtle but serious paint fault.

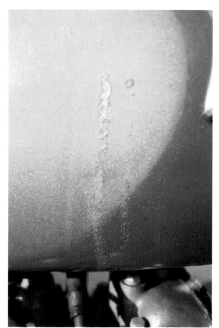

perforation will be found in the metal, and the damage will usually be worse than that suggested by the area of blistering. The metal will have to be repaired before repainting.

Micro blistering

Usually the result of an economy respray where inadequate heating has allowed moisture to settle on the vehicle before spraying. Consult a paint specialist, but damaged paint will have to be removed before partial or full respraying. Can also be caused by bike covers that don't 'breathe'.

Fading

Some colours, especially reds, are prone to fading if subject to strong sunlight for long periods without the benefit of polish protection. Sometimes, proprietary paint restorers and/or paint cutting/rubbing compounds will retrieve the situation. Often, though, a respray is the only real solution.

Peeling

Often a problem with metallic paintwork when the sealing lacquer becomes damaged and begins to peel off. Poorly applied paint may also peel. The remedy is to strip and start again.

Dimples

Dimples in the paintwork are caused by the residue of polish (particularly silicone types) not being removed properly before respraying. Paint removal and repainting is the only solution.

Fuel stains like this should polish out.

15 Problems due to lack of use
– just like their owners, Bonnies need exercise!

Like any piece of engineering, and indeed like human beings, Triumph twins deterioriate if they sit doing nothing for long periods. Especially relevant if the bike is laid up for six months of the year, as some classic bikes are.

Rust
If the bike is put away wet, and/or stored a cold, damp garage, the paint, metal and brightwork will suffer. Ensure the machine is completely dry and clean before going into storage, and if you can afford it, invest in a dehumidifier to keep the garage atmosphere dry.

Rust isn't the end of the world, but it doesn't look good.

Even locked garages get damp.

Seized components
Pistons in brake calipers can seize partially or fully, giving binding or non-working brakes. Cables are vulnerable to seizure, too – the answer is to thoroughly lube them beforehand, and go into the garage to give them a couple of pulls once a week or so.

Tyres
If the bike's been left on its side-stand, most of its weight is on the tyres, which will develop flat spots and cracks over time. Always leave the bike on its centre-stand, which takes weight off the tyres.

Engine
Old, acidic oil can corrode bearings. Many riders change the oil in the spring, when they're putting the bike back on the road, but really it should be

Operate the levers once a week.

Tyres crack and 'set' over time.

changed just before the bike is laid up, so that the bearings are sitting in fresh oil. The same goes for the gearbox. While you're giving the cables their weekly exercise, turn the engine over slowly on the kickstart, ignition off. Don't start it, though – running the engine for a short time does more harm than good, as it produces a lot of moisture internally, which the engine doesn't get hot enough to burn off. This moisture will attack the engine internals, and the silencers.

Battery/electrics
Either remove the battery and give it a top-up charge every couple of weeks, or connect it up to a battery top-up device, such as the Optimate, which will keep it permanently fully charged. Damp conditions will allow fuses and earth connections to corrode, storing up electrical troubles for the spring. Eventually, wiring insulation will harden and fail.

16 The Community

– key people, organisations and companies in the Bonneville world

Auctioneers
See Chapter 10.

Clubs across the world
Triumph Owners Motorcycle Club
The original and longest-lived Triumph
club. Offers a bike dating service.
www.tomcc.org

Bonneville Owners Club
Caters for both Meriden and Hinckley
Bonnevilles.
www.bonnevilleowners.com

Triumph Owners Motorcycle Club
– Germany
www.tomcc.de

Triumph Owners Motorcycle Club – New
Zealand
www.tomcc.nz

Triumph International Owners Club
– USA
PO Box 158, Plympton,
Mass 02367-0158
www.members.aol.com

Triumph Owners Motorcycle Club
– Denmark
www.triumphmc.dk

Triumph Owners Motorcycle Club
– Netherlands
www.tocn.info

Triumph Owners Motorcycle Club
– Belgium
www.tomcc.be

Triumph Owners Motorcycle Club
– Norway
www.tomcc-n.com

Triumph Owners Motorcycle Club
– Australia
PO Box 257, Belgrave, 3160
www.tomcc.cjb.net
www.tomcc.com.au

Triumph Owners Motorcycle Club
– Sweden
www.tomccsweden.org

Club Triton – France
www.triton-france.com

Specialists
There are so many Triumph twin
specialists out there that it would be
impossible to list them all, so we have
restricted our listing to UK companies.
   This list does not imply
recommendation and is not deemed to
be comprehensive.

Allan Jeffries
Spares – Yorkshire
01274 776077

Britbits
Spares – Bournemouth
www.britbits.co.uk
01202 483675

Camelford Bike Bits
Spares – Cornwall
01840 213483

Carl Rosner
Spares – London
www.carlrosner.co.uk
020 8657 0121

High Gear Engine Centre
Engine rebuilds – Surrey
020 8942 2868

Hughie Hancox
Engine rebuilds – Warwickshire
www.hughiehancoxrestorations.co.uk
07773 591694

Kidderminster Motorcycles
Spares – Herefordshire
01562 66679

Kirby Rowbotham
Electronic ignition/oil filters –
Staffordshire
www.kirbyrowbotham.com
01889 584758

LF Harris International
Spares – Devon
Unit 1, Silverhills Road, Decoy Industrial
Estate, Newton Abbot, Devon
TQ12 5ND
01626 369700

Morgo
Uprated oil pumps
www.morgo.co.uk

Norman Hyde
Spares – West Midlands
01926 497375

Reg Allen
Spares – London
www.reg-allen-london.co.uk
020 8579 1248

Richard Hacker Motorcycles
Spares – London
www.richardhacker.co.uk
020 8659 4045

Robin James Engineering
Restorations – Herefordshire
www.robinjamesengineering.com
01568 612800

Rockerbox
Spares – Surrey
01252 722973

Roebuck Motorcycles
Spares – London
020 8868 1231

SRM Engineering
Spares/engineering – Aberystwyth
www.srm-engineering.com
01970 627771

The Bike Shed
Restorations/servicing – Hertfordshire
www.thebikeshed.co.uk
01920 830931

Tri-Supply
Spares – Honiton, Devon
www.trisupply.co.uk
01404 47001

Unity Equipe
Spares – Lancashire
www.unityequipe.com - 01706 632237

Vale Onslow Motorcycles
Spares – Birmingham
www.vale-onslow.co.uk
0121 772 2062

Books

Bonnie: The Development History of the Triumph Bonneville
J R Nelson, Haynes, 1979

British Motorcycles Since 1950 Vols 5 & 6
Steve Wilson, PSL 1992

Illustrated Triumph Motorcycle Buyers Guide
Roy Bacon, Niton, 1989

Tales of Triumph Motorcycles & the Meriden Factory
Hughie Hancox
Veloce

Triumph Pre Unit Twins
Haynes Service & Repair Manual no 0251

Triumph 650 & 750 Unit Twins
Haynes Service & Repair Manual no 0122

Triumph Bonneville Superprofile
Ivor Davies, Haynes

Triumph Twin Restoration
Osprey, Roy Bacon, 1985

Triumph Twins & Triples
Roy Bacon, Osprey, 1981

17 Vital statistics
– essential data at your fingertips

Listing the vital statistics of every Bonneville variant would take far more space than we have available here, so we've picked three representative models: 1959 pre-unit T120, 1968 unit T120, and 1979 T140E.

Max speed
1959 T120 – 108mph
1968 T120 – 110mph
1978 T140 – 113mph

Engine
1959 T120 – Air-cooled vertical twin – 649cc. Bore and stroke 71 x 82mm. Compression ratio 8.5:1. 46bhp @ 6500rpm
1968 T120 – Air-cooled vertical twin – 649cc. Bore and stroke 71 x 82mm. Compression ratio 9:1. 47bhp @ 6700rpm
1979 T140 – Air-cooled vertical twin – 747cc. Bore and stroke 76 x 82mm. Compression ratio 7.9:1. 49bhp @ 6500rpm

Gearbox
1959 T120 – Four-speed. Ratios: 1st 11.20:1; 2nd 7.75:1; 3rd 5.45:1; 4th 4.57:1
1968 T120 – Four-speed. Ratios: 1st 11.81:1; 2nd 8.17:1; 3rd 5.76:1; 4th 4.84:1
1979 T140E – Five-speed. Ratios: 1st 12.23:1; 2nd 8.63:1; 3rd 6.58:1; 4th 5.59:1, 5th 4.70:1

Brakes
1959 T120 – Cable, 8in front drum, 7in rear drum
1968 T120 – Cable, 8in TLS front drum, 7in rear drum
1979 T140E – Hydraulic, 10in discs front and rear

Electrics
1959 T120 – 6-volt, magneto
1968 T120 – 12-volt, alternator
1979 T140E – 12-volt, 3-phase alternator

Weight
1959 T120 – 404lb
1968 T120 – 363lb (1963)
1978 T140 – 395lb

Major change points by model years
1959 Bonneville T120 launched
1960 Duplex frame, alternator, chrome headlight shell
1961 Strengthened frame, standard Amal Monoblocs
1962 Larger alternator, heavier flywheel
1963 Unit construction, single downtube frame

1964 New forks, Thruxton launched (this year only)

1965 Revised forks

1966 New frame geometry, 12-volt electrics, bigger oil tank, bigger front brake

1967 New oil pump, E3134 inlet cam

1968 TLS front brake, 6CA contact breakers, two-way damped forks, braced swingarm, stroboscopic timing cover, finned zener diode under headlight, Amal Concentric carbs

1969 Heavier flywheel, UNF threads, RM21 alternator

1970 New engine breathing system

1971 New generation – oil-in-frame, conical hub drum brakes, Ceriani-style alloy forks, indicators, squared-off UK-spec fuel tank, restyled sidepanels, skimpy mudguards

1972 Lowered frame/seat height, five-speed gearbox option, new cylinder head with finned rocker caps

1973 T140 launched, front disc brake

1974 Lower 7.9:1 compression ratio, US-spec offered in UK

1975 No changes due to factory blocade

1976 Left-foot gearchange, rear disc brake

1977 Silver Jubilee, Girling gas rear shocks

1978 Improved oil-tightness, Yuasa battery, new seat

1979 T140E launched with parallel twin Amal carbs, timing-side roller bearing, Lucas Rita electronic ignition, three-phase alternator, new Lucas switchgear, lockable seat, rear parcel rack, T140D Special offered

1980 Bonneville Executive launched, four-valve oil pump, Avon Roadrunner tyres, Electro electric start option

1981 Higher gearing, inlet valve oil seals, Royal Wedding Bonneville offered, twin AP Racing front discs optional, Bing CV carbs, Marzocchi remote reservoir rear shocks

1982 TSS and TSX launched, Meriden co-op closes at end of 1982

June 1985 Harris Bonneville launched with Paioli forks, Brembo brakes (twin front discs), Magura switchgear, Lafranconi silencers

March 1988 Production ends

Engine/frame numbers

Production for each model year began in August. That is, 1969 model bikes began rolling off the lines in August 1968, after the summer holidays. T120 or T140 suffix after the engine/frame number denotes 650 or 750 Bonneville respectively.

1959	020076-029363
1960	D101-D7726
1961	D7727-D15788
1962	D15789 on
1963	DU101-DU5824
1964	DU5825-DU13374
1965	DU13375-DU24874
1966	DU24875-DU44393
1967	DU44394-DU66245
1968	DU66246-DU85903

From 1969, the first letter denoted the month of build and the second the model year, as follows:

	Month		Model Year
A	January	C	1969
B	February	D	1970
C	March	E	1971
D	April	G	1972
E	May	H	1973
G	June	J	1974
H	July	K	1975
J	August	N	1976
K	September	P	1977
N	October	X	1978
P	November	B	1980
X	December	KDA	1981
		EDA	1982
		BEA	1983

1970 KD7866 on
1971 KE00001 on
1972 HG30870 on
1973 T120 – JH15597 on
T140 (724cc) – JH15435-XH22018
T140 (744cc) – XH22019 on
1974 T120 – GJ55101-KJ59067
T140 – GJ55101-NJ60032
1975 T120 – to NJ60070
T140 – to EK62239

1976 HN62501 on
1977 GP75000 on
1978 HX00100 on
1979 HA11001 on
1980 PB25001 on
1981 KDA28001 on
1982 EDA30001 on
1983 BEA33001-AEA34393
1985 00001
1986 to SN001258

Suffix letters denote model variants as follows:
A US market, road (1960)
B US market, competition (1960)
R US market, road (also used in UK some years)
RT US market-only 750 (1970)
C US market, competition (high-level exhausts)
V Five-speed gearbox
E Confirms to US environmental rules
ES Electric start
D Bonneville Special (1979-80)
TSS Eight-valve engine
TSX US-style custom
LE Royal limited edition (1982)
AV Police frame (originally 'anti-vibration')

The **Essential** Buyer's Guide™

The Essential Buyer's Guide
ALFA ROMEO GIULIA
GT COUPE

978-1-904788-69-0

The Essential Buyer's Guide
ALFA ROMEO GIULIA
SPIDER

978-1-904788-98-0

The Essential Buyer's Guide
BSA
500 & 650 Twins
A7, A10, A50 & A65: 1946 to 1973

978-1-84584-136-2

The Essential Buyer's Guide
CITROËN
DS & ID
All models
1966 to 1975

978-1-84584-138-6

The Essential Buyer's Guide
CITROËN
2CV

978-1-845840-99-0

The Essential Buyer's Guide
MERCEDES-BENZ
280-560SL & SLC
W107 series Roadsters & Coupés
1971 to 1989

978-1-845841-07-2

The Essential Buyer's Guide
MG
MGB
MGB GT

978-1-845840-29-7

The Essential Buyer's Guide
MORRIS
MINOR & 1000
Saloons, Travellers & Convertibles
1952 to 1971

978-1-845841-01-0

The Essential Buyer's Guide
PORSCHE
928

978-1-904788-70-6

The Essential Buyer's Guide
ROLLS-ROYCE
SILVER SHADOW
BENTLEY
T-SERIES
Including Corniche, Camargue, Silver
Shadow II & Bentley T-2: 1965 to 1995

978-1-84584-146-1

The Essential Buyer's Guide
JAGUAR
E-type
V12 5.3 litre

978-1845840-77-8

The Essential Buyer's Guide
JAGUAR
E-type
3.8 & 4.2 litre

978-1-904788-85-0

The Essential Buyer's Guide
FIAT
500 & 600 1955 to 1992
Saloons/Sedans, Multipla, Giardiniera & 126

978-1-84584-147-8

The Essential Buyer's Guide
JAGUAR/DAIMLER
XJ6, XJ12
& Sovereign
All Jaguar/Daimler/VDP series I, II & III
models 1968 to 1992

978-1-845841-19-5

The Essential Buyer's Guide
MERCEDES-BENZ 'PAGODA'
230, 250 & 280SL
W113 series Roadsters & Coupés
1963 to 1971

978-1-845841-13-3

The Essential Buyer's Guide
SUBARU
Impreza
All turbo models 1994 to 2007

978-1-84584-163-8

The Essential Buyer's Guide
BMW
GS

978-1-845841-34-8

The Essential Buyer's Guide
Triumph
TR6

978-1-845840-26-6

The Essential Buyer's Guide
VOLKSWAGEN
BEETLE

978-1-904788-72-0

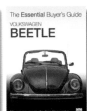

The Essential Buyer's Guide
VOLKSWAGEN
BUS

978-1-845840-22-8

£9.99*/$19.95*

*prices subject to change. p&p extra. for more details visit www.veloce.co.uk or email info@veloce.co.uk.

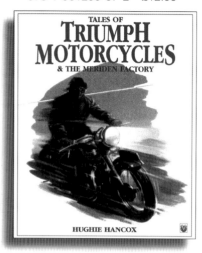
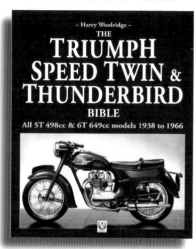
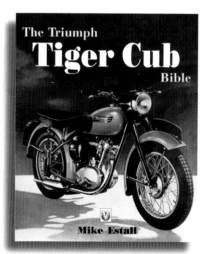
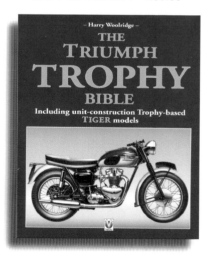

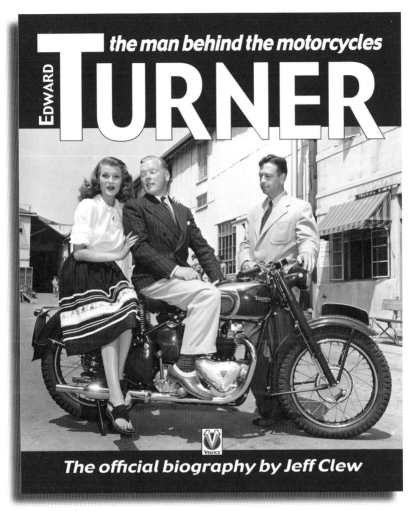

EDWARD *the man behind the motorcycles*
TURNER
The official biography by Jeff Clew

"Turner was an inventive genius who had a flair for pleasing shapes and an uncanny ability to perceive what the buying public would readily accept, to produce it at the right price." For the first time, the life of Edward Turner, one of Britain's most talented motorcycle designers, is revealed in full.

Paperback • 25x20.7cm • £17.99* • 160 pages • 140 colour & b&w photos • ISBN: 978-1-84584-065-5

www.veloce.co.uk

Index